Frank A. Colson, 1975.

by

Kiln Building with Space-Age Materials

Drawings by Nancy Nugent

VNR **VAN NOSTRAND REINHOLD COMPANY**
New York Cincinnati Toronto London Melbourne

Dedicated to Artist-Craftsmen Everywhere

Copyright © 1975 by Litton Educational Publishing, Inc.
Library of Congress Catalog Card Number 75-3972
ISBN 0-442-21641-6   (cloth)

Designed by Loudan Enterprises

Published in 1975 by Van Nostrand Reinhold Company
A Division of Litton Educational Publishing, Inc.
450 West 33rd Street
New York, NY 10001, U.S.A.
Van Nostrand Reinhold Limited
1410 Birchmount Road
Scarborough, Ontario M1P 2E7, Canada
Van Nostrand Reinhold Australia Pty. Ltd.
17 Queen Street
Mitcham, Victoria 3132, Australia
Van Nostrand Reinhold Company Ltd.
Molly Millars Lane
Wokingham, Berkshire, England

16 15 14 13 12 11 10 9 8 7 6 5 4 3 2 1

Library of Congress Cataloging in Publication Data
Colson, Frank A
  Kiln building with space-age materials.

  1. Kilns. 2. Fibrous composites. I. Title.
ISBN 0-442-21641-6

A modified Saturn V rocket, topped by the Skylab space station, represents the result of advanced technology from which space-age kilns
eventually developed.

Contents

Acknowledgments

My special thanks to my wife, Diana, for editing this material in spite of it not being on the X-rated list. To Brooke Andrews for her diligence in staying in the dark room for so many hours. To Bill Hines for scorching his eyebrows shooting the color photo.

My additional thanks to Nancy Nugent for working closely with me on the many details of the line drawings which she has executed so well.

Lastly, my thanks to John Nicol for working up the methane gas production plant chart, and to Union Carbide for their contribution on new systems of gas production from solid waste matter.

Foreword

Since the development of new materials, made possible through massive funds and limitless research, a number of products have emerged which drastically change the basic approach toward kiln construction and firing techniques. No longer is it necessary to think in terms of heavy, bulky kilns which require huge amounts of fuel input to create the proper heat conditions for bringing clay to maturity and glazes to flow.

New approaches are necessary to go along with the manner in which these revolutionary materials are used and how they can serve the objective of the craftsman.

All too frequently the artist-craftsman has limited his creativity solely to the aesthetics of his work, not extending this creativity to the equipment so essential to his craft, in spite of the many possibilities offered in this age of advanced technology. The information in this book is primarily aimed at showing the individual artist-craftsman how to use new materials in the construction of pottery kilns. These materials have been in existence for nearly two decades, so there is no question of their availability; it is only a matter of applying the new material once its nature is understood.

In a world of shrinking resources, where natural fuels are becoming severely limited and more expensive, the most immediate solution is to develop new kilns which are considerably more efficient in operation and use of heat than the traditional kilns of the past. The new materials described in this book provide the means to develop such new kilns, and several "new" kilns are discussed in the following chapters.

Introduction: Space-Age Materials

In the developmental stage of the United States space program, it was evident that it would be virtually impossible for a rocket to be launched off of its pad if its firebox was lined with conventional firebricks. Materials had to be developed with extremely high heat insulating qualities combined with practically no weight. Because of this need, great effort was made during the sixties to develop and manufacture new materials for space vehicles. Although some of these sophisticated, high heat tolerance materials were not readily available for application outside of the space program, other materials were easily adaptable to such industrial markets as steel tempering furnaces, boiler insulations, glass-conveying roll covers, and reactor insulation. Born to meet specialized needs in the space program, these space-age materials can often replace traditional refractory materials.

As an individual who stands apart from the industrial market, the artist-craftsman may be the last to learn about application of the new refractory materials. Unable to afford the time and money spent by industry to research and develop applications for such materials, he nonetheless would greatly benefit from adapting these materials to his own personal use. The purpose of this book is to make the potter aware of the many possibilities for using these materials in new kilns.

What are the new materials and how do they work to make a better kiln for the potter? To date there exists no comprehensive catalogue or bibliography of them, but in the few short years they have been commercially available, they have undergone a great deal of development and improvement. Therefore, it is important to know which refractory materials are currently available on the open market, and to understand their basic differences.

Among the most available and diversified of the materials are the alumina-silica ceramic fibers. Although there are several other types of ceramic fibers made from zirconium, quartz, and other minerals tolerant to high temperatures, the alumina-silica fibers are the most easily available and reasonably priced. Weighing one-fortieth the equivalent volume of firebrick, these materials have a normal heat exposure range of 2,300°F. Quite recently, new fibers containing 20 percent more alumina have been developed which have a working temperature of 2,600°F., well within the potter's heat range for stoneware temperatures. One manufacturer is presently developing an alumina-silica fiber with a heat tolerance above 2600°F.

Alumina-silica-based fibers occasionally have small additions of soda borax or zirconia as modifiers to make the material more stable.

Another family of ceramic fibers is based on zirconium oxide. The element zircon is used extensively in the ceramics industry by itself, in refractory compounds, and as an alloying agent in nuclear reactors. Its melting point is extremely high. To manufacture zirconium ceramic fibers requires very high temperatures, and, as a result, a very sophisticated insulating material is produced that can be exposed to a constant heat of 3,000°F. Zircon-based ceramic fibers are commercially available and although they are costly, are not altogether prohibitive if application demands them.

An even more sophisticated ceramic fiber is the boron-nitrate-based material, which is extracted from kernite and borax. It has an extremely high melt point which makes it usable continuously at temperatures of 4,500°F. Although these fibers, which are often used for nuclear reactor control elements, are the best of their type commercially available, high cost is a very definite factor in considering their use.

Among other ceramic fibers produced for their extremely fine insulating qualities are those made from quartz and nickel. However, these types of fibers are limited to use in components of space vehicles, and are not available commercially.

In every case, regardless of the mineral from which they are produced, the ceramic fibers have extremely wide-ranging properties. They do not go through the physical changes of expansion and contraction when used within their prescribed heat limitations. They have excellent thermal insulation characteristics, low heat capacity, are extremely light in weight, are unaffected by heat shock, show resistance to flame erosion, and are chemically inert and thus not affected by either oxidation or reduction firings. They are also exceptionally resistant to wetting, have no outgassing, and are completely inorganic in composition. The manufacturer, however, will often put some organic binders into the material during fabrication in order to add durability for handling and installation, but these usually are made to burn out after initial exposure to heat. Other nonorganic binders which help to maintain the shape and stability of the ceramic fiber during use provide a wide range of ceramic-fiber forms.

Alumina-silica ceramic-fiber products are produced by melting white alumina ore along with flint and borax glass to a temperature of 3,600°F. in an electrical furnace. A jet of steam blasts the molten material as it is poured, and this produces a fluffy, white, bulk ceramic-fiber which ranges up to 10 microns in diameter and 1½ inches in length. This ceramic fiber can be used to produce blanket, block, board, bulk fiber, casting mixes, liquid cements, felts, paper, spray mix, tamping mixes, textiles, tubes, vacuum-cast shapes, and numerous other forms. The ceramic fibers that are basic to these forms interlock to maintain structural integrity and thus remain strong and resilient. Since there is no brittle structure to develop stresses during sudden chilling, the result is a superior thermal product which has flexibility of usage and application.

Although alumina-silica fiber was made experimentally in 1942, it wasn't until 1952 that it became available on the open market. Since that time ceramic fibers have been placed under numerous patents, and countless different forms based on the composition and processes have been developed in recent years.

In 1974 the Federal Power Commission forecast a "severe crisis" for natural gas availability in the future. The commission chairman reported that there is no end to natural gas shortages in the immediate future and that "many large and giant new fields must be found and developed with regularity to improve the supply position." Since ceramic fibers do not require natural gas for production methods, as do traditional refractory materials like firebricks, it is evident that these materials will become the prevailing product available for the potter to use in the construction of his kiln of the future.

The conventional approach to kiln construction remains rigidly based on long tradition and firing methods on the use of traditional materials for which known predictabilities have been established. With the use of new materials to achieve the same end, it becomes necessary to develop a very different way of thinking about kilns. The function of ceramic-fiber products can most easily be understood when they are used as a secondary means of application in conjunction with traditional refractory bricks, since in this usage they simply improve the manner in which bricks perform. For this reason, the use of new materials as a supplement to brick is illustrated in chapters 2 and 3; both chapters present high-temperature brick kilns which are designed with a ceramic-fiber blanket as secondary insulation. (Each of the different kilns discussed in chapters 2 to 7 has accompanying diagrams showing exact measurements along with a materials list at the end of the chapter.)

Since ceramic-fiber thermal materials became available, I have been using them as an integrated part of many kilns both for myself and other craftsmen. First I used the alumina-silica "blanket" as a partial replacement for bricks, and this alone cut fuel costs to one-fourth, firing time to one-third, and labor and materials to one-half for high-temperature reduction kilns. Later, in addition to the blanket, I used other forms of alumina-silica fiber materials in specialized areas, such as burner ports, fireboxes, flue boxes, and doors on kilns made of brick.

When kilns are made entirely out of ceramic fibers—without any use of brick—the pattern of reflection and retention of heat is different; therefore, it is necessary to understand and allow for these differences when firing. This concept is discussed in chapters 4, 5, 6, and 7, each of which deals with a different type of ceramic-fiber kiln. Each kiln has been proven in operation many times over.

Chapter 8 describes the different forms of ceramic fibers and binders—such as cement, liquid rigidizer, blanket, board, casting mixes—and how to use them to repair and operate conventional kilns. In addition, several kiln systems using vacuum-formed shapes are discussed as a preview of manufactured kilns of the future.

No attempt has been made to depict the construction of an electric kiln since the same basic principles of insulation apply whether the kiln is fired by electricity or fuel. However, the fuel kiln has many variables related to heat input, whereas the electric kiln is quite predictable once the current is flowing through the heating coils. The variables encountered in operating a fuel kiln, particularly one made of ceramic fibers, can sometimes affect reaching temperature, controlling reduction, and handling flame effects. Many of these variables are discussed in chapter 9, "Trouble Shooting."

The last chapter, "Safety Regulations and Pollution-Control Fuel Systems," covers some of the realities you face when placing a kiln in an area of restrictive zoning as well as the pollution problems encountered during some kiln firings. With regard to this last matter, the fuels which generate the heat for a kiln are factors of no small importance. A complete methane production flow chart is given along with suggestions about the development of fuels of the future. The nature of his work makes the artist-craftsman sensitive to future technological developments. I hope the material in this chapter will inspire the reader to develop solutions in the field of self-generating energy for space-age kilns of the future.

1. Kilns: Theory and Practice

In order to achieve the desired firing result, a potter must have some understanding of basic types of fuel kilns. With gas kilns, the effect desired is usually accomplished by means of a so-called "reduction firing" rather than oxidizing a kiln during the firing cycle—the norm with electric kilns. The term "reduction firing" is commonly used in contemporary pottery shop talk, and very simply implies that the oxygen in the atmosphere of a kiln is *reduced,* thus starving the flame of its natural fuel. Since there is little oxygen within the kiln on which the flame can feed, it goes after particles of minerals and chemicals within the clay and glazes of the pottery. The result is that the iron impurities in the clay body come to the surface and "bleed" on the face of the glaze. Iron glazes turn green (and are referred to as "celadon"), while copper-based glazes turn red (reduction red, or "oxblood"); the general effect of the pottery is much different than that obtained with oxidation firing in electric kilns.

Since reduction firing requires what most industrial gas servicemen refer to as a "dirty" flame, it is easy to understand why this firing method is more of an art than a set of procedures. Each kiln has its own distinctive firing characteristics. Furthermore, each potter must discover his particular kiln's traits and learn to work with them in order to have successful firings. Success cannot be achieved with one firing alone; ten firings of the same kiln may only begin to bring the consistent control that the potter desires.

Most kilns come under two general categories—updraft and downdraft—and each type has its own set of advantages and disadvantages for reduction firing. Almost all fuel-fired kilns built today are designed so as to allow ample flame circulation within and around the stack area where pottery is placed. But this was not the case some years ago when the "flashing" which occurs due to a flame lick was not considered an aesthetic attribute on a pot. Because of this, kilns were designed and built with complete baffle chambers around the entire stack area so as to prevent flames from even remotely approaching the ware. In some cases, kiln designs provided for each burner flame to pass through a ceramic tube in the kiln, from the bottom to the top. These kilns were referred to as "muffle kilns," since they muffled the flame and used the heat that radiated through the ceramic tubes to reach the needed temperature. The atmosphere of these kilns was clear and clean, and oxidation firing was the only condition. However, with fuel kilns which are not muffled, freer flame circulation within the stack area allows more direct heat penetration from the flame, consequently less fuel is required, resulting in savings to the potter. Direct flame exposure also changes the effect of the glazes, creating warm, pleasant differences rarely available with a muffle kiln.

Updraft Kilns

Most commercially built fuel kilns on the market today are updraft kilns, primarily because of the simplicity of building such a kiln as well as packing and shipping it. An updraft kiln consists of two basic elements which contribute to the simplicity of its design: the first is a firebox,

10

where most of the flame is concentrated, and which is always located on the floor directly under the bottom shelf of the stack area. The second is the flue-damper system where the flame exhaust is controlled; this is actually a part of the top of the kiln and consists of little more than a hole in the roof.

In some cases, the burner system for an updraft kiln is located under the structure, pointing upward. But sometimes the system is on the side or even the back in a horizontal position. Such a kiln may also have burners within it located at floor level. Regardless of the burners' placement, the direction of the flame in an updraft kiln always commences at floor level and goes up through the kiln and out of the flue opening on top. This being so, the problem is to acquire the best efficiency of flame while the flame is in the kiln and to control it for reduction. When the flame enters the kiln at the firebox, it makes its primary circulation. The objective, then, is to hold as much as possible of this flame within the kiln before it is drawn up and out of the flue on top of the kiln. This can be done by placing a small wedge-shaped brick in front of the burners inside the kiln.

Depending upon where and how such a brick is placed, flame can be directed inward toward the center of the firebox or in another direction of more efficient use. The flame is split up into segments and directed into areas that might not otherwise be covered in the firebox. Burners that enter through the sides of a kiln may have such circulation devices, while kilns with burners directed vertically from underneath are often baffled with a refractory plate located a few inches above the burner openings within. In the latter case, the flame, which is dispersed out over the firebox bottom, spreads the heat as evenly as possible. These devices, as well as the density with which the ware is stacked, affect the length of time that the heat of the flame is held within the kiln. With experience in firing as well as stacking a kiln, you will be able to determine the flame's best level of efficiency.

Initial reduction during the firing cycle will depend upon the amount and type of flame that goes into the firebox. If an overabundance of fuel is pushed into the updraft kiln, the draft system will simply accelerate the passage of the flame through the kiln and out the flue, with the result that proper fuel combustion (the right amount of air and raw flame) will take place outside the kiln at the point where the flame leaves the flue. One of several signs indicating combustion is going on outside rather than inside the kiln

is difficulty in gaining temperature. You can usually notice this by the excess time and fuel comsumption required for firing. Another indication will be the extremely active flame coming out of the flue, often in the form of fiercely waving tails along with a low muffled sound of roaring fire. What is deceiving is that this type of flame will often present a great deal of smoke, leading the potter to believe that a good reduction is taking place. It *is*—but outside the kiln! If these effects are encountered early in the firing cycle, before cone 06 for instance, there often is a distinct odor of carbon dioxide which tends to smart the nasal passages and indicates incorrect fuel combustion. The object, then, is to set up the flame input and the damper control so as to make combustion occur within the kiln. This will bring about a heat rise, thus making possible the conditions needed for a reducing atmosphere.

Unlike a downdraft kiln, an updraft kiln has no chimney stack; its one great advantage in reduction firing, therefore, is that there is a means of seeing and controlling the amount of reduction. Excessive reduction, which also produces excessive back-pressure within the kiln, will result in an extensive flame (more than 12 inches) coming out of the top of the flue. Thus the flame that you see coming out of the flue and the way you adjust your kiln settings for that flame are the most important factors in a successful firing.

In the early cycle of firing an updraft kiln (before heat color occurs), the burners are kept soft and low so as to confine the flame within the boundaries of the firebox. Flame from the burners should not be allowed to lick against any pots until after all the chemical water has been removed (500°F. to 900°F.). The damper is wide open at this point. Once the temperature has passed beyond 900°F., you may close the damper nearly three-quarters while bringing the flame up more and more during the early stages of the firing cycle. The function of this damper position is to hold as much heat in the kiln as possible during the early oxidizing stages of firing. Once color in the kiln has begun, you can pay close attention to the flue on top the kiln.

It is helpful to plan the timing of a firing so that color within the kiln will coincide with dusk or early evening; darkness will facilitate seeing flame emerge from the flue. If the first flame out of the flue appears blue, this will indicate that the temperature within the kiln is not yet high enough to prompt proper reduction conditions. At this point, the damper should be opened substantially, which will result either in a disappearance of any visible flame or a change in color from blue to orange-yellow. As heat continues to build up within the kiln and fuel input continues (up to the point of greatest efficiency, so as not to push fuel through the kiln), the flame coming out of the flue will increase. Once you can see a strong orange color within the kiln—anywhere from cone 08 to 01—reduction should begin. A visible flame should be coming from the flue now: orange, about 12 inches long, and very active. If viewing conditions are good, you may observe a small amount of smoke coming off the top of the flame, and this should indicate that the type of flame going through the kiln is naturally smoky from the burners right through to the flue opening. When you reach the high-temperature range of the firing cycle—cone five and above—check the kind of flame coming out of the flue often.

Make damper adjustments as needed. The greater the fuel input into the kiln, the more important it is to look at the color and kind of flame coming out of the flue. The back pressure of fuel in the kiln is kept in check by adjusting the flue damper opening. This damper is the primary device for controlling proper combustion, sufficient reduction, and the increase of heat, once the fuel input is at a constant setting.

During the peak of the firing, a secondary characteristic of proper reduction may be observed: the accumulation of slight carbon deposits around the peepholes in the door and around the damper openings.

Summarizing the advantages of an updraft kiln: First and foremost, it is simple to construct, being nothing more than a refractory box in which there is a fuel input in one end and a fuel outlet on the other. Also, with such a kiln, the characteristics of reduction firing can be observed through the entire firing cycle, making it relatively easy to learn reduction firing techniques that can be controlled with considerable consistency.

Downdraft Kilns

A distinct advantage of the downdraft kiln is that it uses fuel more efficiently than the updraft. However, firing for reduction is a more complex operation. The downdraft kiln consists of three basic structural elements: the firebox, where fuel combustion takes place; the stack area, where pots are placed; and the kiln stack, which includes the flue damper system. Since the basic principle of a downdraft kiln entails directing flame downward inside the kiln, and not upward, the firebox is usually a separate section, lo-

cated apart from the pottery stack area. Whereas in some kiln designs the firebox is on one side of the kiln, in other designs it may be split up into two or more areas on opposite sides of the kiln. The stack is also built as a separate structure apart from the kiln itself. Sometimes it may be tangent to the kiln in the rear or on the side, but in some cases it is several feet away. The function of this stack is to create a draft for the flame in the firebox so that the flame is drawn through the ware in the stack area. This draft commences either under the kiln floor or on the same level as the floor.

The height of the stack or chimney, plus its diameter, must be directly related to the size of the kiln if the proper draft is to be created. For the purpose of reduction, fuel back pressure within the kiln is controlled with the damper, which is located at the bottom of the kiln stack. The damper is handled in much the same manner as for updraft kilns, but it is important to understand other characteristics of a downdraft kiln in order to control reduction during the firing cycle.

Since the firebox in a downdraft kiln is normally separate from the pottery stack area, you must allow time in the early portion of the firing cycle for the firebox area to be heated. This must be done before the ware area will reach any substantial temperature. At the onset of a firing it may be difficult to acquire even a little draft within the kiln to draw the flame up from the burners because the kiln stack may be at some distance from the firebox. One actual advantage of such a firebox arrangement, however, is that the ware is protected from being licked by flame in the early part of the firing cycle. Once heat has begun to build up within the kiln, a substantial draft will usually occur if the damper is wide open. As heat continues to build up, with the damper set to maintain the greatest fuel efficiency as described earlier, you must watch for the signs of reduction conditions.

The first indication of reduction is in the kiln atmosphere itself. If when you look into the kiln, the inside is hazy or foggy, this means there is smoke inside the chamber and indicates reduction. It is difficult to observe obvious signs of reduction in a downdraft kiln—particularly in the early firing stages. In order to make these signs plainer, however, you can close down the damper control, thus creating a little more back pressure than necessary. When you do this, a forceful carbonization will take place around the peephole, and if you open a peephole (particularly a top peep), a forceful smoky flame will leap out. At this point, the back pressure should be let up a little by opening the damper slightly while you observe the nature of the flame from the peeps. The top peep should have a warm yellow-orange flame about six inches long with a very slight smoky tip to it. The middle peep should be the same color, but only about three inches long. The bottom peep will often be neutral—that is, there will neither be a draft (which can be checked by holding a lit match in front of the hole), nor a flame coming out of it to indicate any great back pressure. These conditions should be maintained by making damper adjustments as the heat buildup increases within the kiln and you reach the desired temperature. If at any point during the firing cycle you are uncertain about how reduction conditions are progressing, you can close the damper down a bit to overcompensate for reduction and then readjust by backing off the damper once again.

In making adjustments for reduction effects during a firing, keep in mind that the kiln must have at least a half-hour to make adjustment. It is therefore easy to misjudge what is taking place during the firing if you make damper or fuel adjustments at intervals of less than thirty minutes. In fact, in many cases it is wiser to wait at least an hour between adjustments, but this depends on the size of the kiln, since large kilns take considerably more time to readjust to a setting than small kilns. Perhaps the greatest frustration you can experience in attempting to make a reduction firing comes when you anticipate what the kiln will do without giving it a chance to show its own traits. As already mentioned, it usually takes more than several firings to learn a fuel kiln's traits and to be able to make predictions that will contribute to the control needed for firing. After you have fired a kiln many times, your experience contributes to the predictability of a firing cycle, which, in turn, leads to your needing to give less attention to each firing. Each subsequent firing will then fall into a pattern, which may vary only slightly, according to the manner in which pots are stacked.

In reviewing the advantages of the downdraft kiln, note that although this type is a more complex structure to build and involves a great deal of labor and materials, the way it holds heat by passing the flame down through the ware and out of the floor is very efficient. It is more difficult to reduce with this type of kiln until you have learned and can predict its firing characteristics.

I have tried to make no specific recommendations as to what temperatures begin reduction or oxidation or at what point glazes or clay body are reduced, but have attempted to show instead *how* to set up the conditions for reduction firing with two basic types of kilns, the updraft and the downdraft.

Since the kiln itself is a retaining box for heat, a system that will generate heat must be provided. You must understand burners and the basic types of fuels that burners use in order to reach a given temperature within the kiln. As already noted, kilns constructed with the new materials discussed in the following chapters provide such excellent insulation that the heat input needed is considerably less than for conventional brick kilns and there is a resulting saving of fuel. (Fig. 1–1.)

1–1.

Fuel Comparison Chart

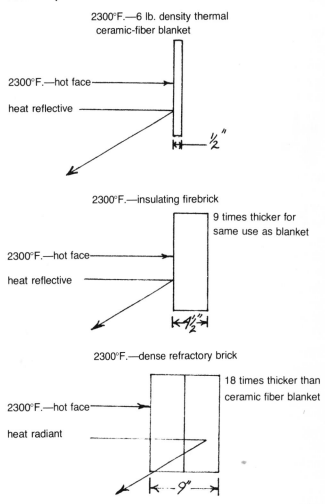

2300°F.—6 lb. density thermal ceramic-fiber blanket

2300°F.—hot face

heat reflective

½"

2300°F.—insulating firebrick

9 times thicker for same use as blanket

2300°F.—hot face

heat reflective

4½"

2300°F.—dense refractory brick

18 times thicker than ceramic fiber blanket

2300°F.—hot face

heat radiant

9"

Since each of the chapters 2 through 7 deals with a specific kiln and has a detailed description of the construction and specifications for the kiln's burner system, no attempt will be made to discuss individual types of burners here. Excellent material on this subject is available in chapter 1 of Daniel Rhodes's book, *Kilns: Design, Construction, and Operation,* as well as in *The Kiln Book* by Frederick Olsen. However, you will need some understanding of the types of burners and the nature of proper combustion, as well as knowledge of some of the side effects which may occur during operation because this information is especially pertinent to space-age kilns with their different heat-control systems.

Combustion

Combustion, the process of combining oxygen with fuel, results in the release of heat. In order to achieve proper combustion, air (which contains oxygen) and fuel are mixed together in a ratio which does not leave excess fuel unburnt or deprive the fuel of an opportunity to burn at its maximum rate. The correct proportion is ten parts of air to one part of fuel (gas). An inadequate quantity of fuel in the mixture results in oxidation because the oxygen in the air is not totally consumed while excess fuel results in a "rich mixture" (or an insufficient amount of oxygen), creating a carbonizing atmosphere and incomplete burning of fuel.

The ignition which initiates combustion occurs when the oxidation reaction (a flame) is induced by an external heat source and the reaction itself releases heat faster than the heat which is lost to its surroundings. Or, to put it another way, after introduction of the external heat source, the heat from the oxidation reaction ignites in what is referred to as "spontaneous combustion."

All measurements of heat are based upon B.t.u. (British thermal unit)—the quantity of heat necessary to raise one pound of water one degree Fahrenheit. The amount of B.t.u. given off by any natural or liquid gas burner is determined by the size of the orifice. The orifice allows a given amount of fuel to pass into the burner chamber, where the fuel is combined with air, and where, when ignited, it creates a flame. A flame may be defined as a zone in which the combustion reaction is occurring at such a rate as to produce visible radiation. The flame front is the place along which combustion starts. When the correct conditions take place, the flame front appears to be stationary, because the flame is moving toward the end of the burner with the same speed that the fuel-air mixture is coming out. (This may be compared with a fish swimming upstream at 5 miles per hour in a 5-mile-per-hour current.)

If the fuel-air mixture is fed into the burner at too fast a rate, the flame may blow off. (Now imagine a fish swimming 5 miles per hour downstream in a 6-mile-per-hour current.) This is identified as a "pop-off" of the flame from the lip of the burner which leaves a gap between the rear end of the flame and the front end of the burner. (Fig. 1–2.) If the fuel-air mixture is fed into the burner at too slow a rate, the flame may have a "flashback" into the burner. (Now the fish is making headway at 5 miles per hour in a 3-mile-per-hour current.) In some extreme cases the flame may flash back as far as the mixing point just above the orifice hole, causing the burner itself, which gets extremely hot, to become the heat chamber for the flame instead of the kiln.

Atmospheric burners using natural or liquid gas (which vaporizes) have two important and basic components which are necessary for successful operation: primary and secondary air control. Although these components are also necessary factors in burners using dense and hard fuels such as oil, coal, and wood, they are more identifiable in burners using gas fuels, where they are easier to control. Note in Figure 1–2 that the primary air is drawn in below the point of ignition.

Burner Fuel-Air Mixture

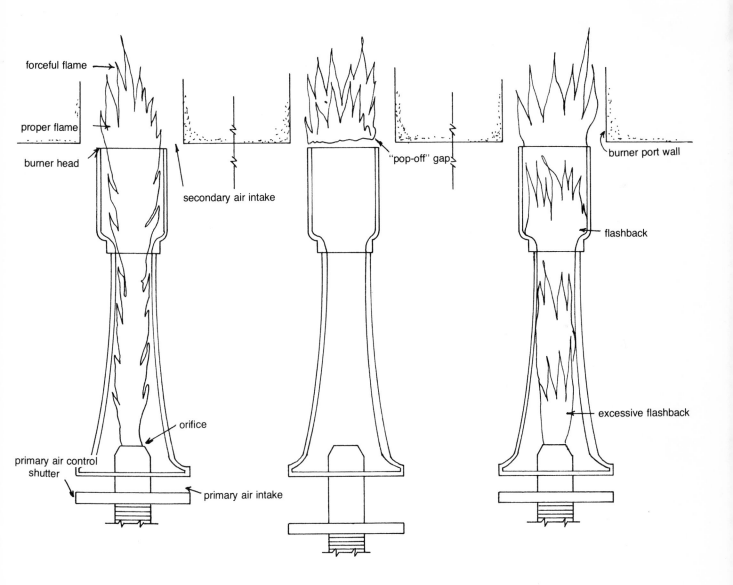

forceful flame

proper flame

burner head

secondary air intake

"pop-off" gap

burner port wall

flashback

orifice

primary air control shutter

primary air intake

excessive flashback

When the primary air combines with the flame at the ignition point of the burner, the cooler air is heated, and as a result the flame increases in velocity, creating a forceful driving flame at the burner tip. This basic principle, known as the Venturi effect, is the same one that powers a jet engine on a 747. The secondary air is that which combines with the flame at the tip of the burner where proper combustion is taking place and is being driven into the kiln. An excessive amount of secondary air at this location creates a "cool" flame going into the kiln, and insufficient secondary air creates a flame lacking in proper combustion, which results in a reducing or smoky flame.

Primary air is controlled by the air shutter located near the orifice head—secondary air by the position of the burner head in the burner port.

For any given burner, a change in the fuel-mixture pressure or the amount of primary air will affect the flame shape. Increase in fuel pressure will broaden the flame in most burners while an increase in the primary air will shorten the flame (assuming the input rate remains the same). But the design of the burner has much more effect upon flame length and shape than either of these operating variables. Good mixing, produced by a high degree of turbulence and velocity, creates a short bushy flame, whereas poor (delayed) mixing and low velocity result in a long, slender flame. Interestingly, burners may be ignited at the point of their external heat termination (the end of the burner). If the position of the burner is correct, initial combustion occurs only at this point, often leaving the internal area of the burner totally without flame. Although this creates a soft flowing flame rather than one which has velocity, this flame serves its purpose well by creating a reduction atmosphere within the kiln and still providing necessary heat rise.

Another type of burner which does not operate by using atmospheric air as a part of its mixing procedure is the forced-air burner. This type burner does not require a secondary air intake since the air is being forced into the burner chamber by mechanical means. With this burner, a much greater fuel input into the chamber of the burner is possible, and its flame, which is very forceful, enables a massive amount of B.t.u. to be thrust into the kiln chamber.

It should be noted that burners designed for operation at sea level may not work as efficiently at high altitudes, where there is less oxygen in the air. At 8,000-feet altitude there is nearly 20 percent less free oxygen present than at sea level, so that atmospheric burners need greater primary air to work properly and to provide the necessary B.t.u. In some cases, you may have to change from atmospheric to forced-air burners.

Oil burners of various types work most efficiently with a forced-air blower system. However, some oil burners are designed to operate without forced air and yet are able to provide an extremely powerful flame, as if forced air were being used. An example of this type is the oil burner which operates by converting oil into a vapor under pressure before it is released at the orifice opening. Naturally, this burner does not require any electrical means to create its forceful flame. Figures 1–3 and 1–4 illustrate a unique burner of this type that is used extensively in Guadalajara, Mexico, for heating the numerous glass furnaces where hand-blown glass is made.

After you have acquired a basic understanding of burners, it is important that you become aware of the effect that flame has upon that area of the kiln where heat input is being initiated—the area universally referred to as the "firebox."

The firebox, of course, is the heat energy source for the entire kiln; it is the motor which makes the kiln go! Firebox shapes and sizes may differ, according to the type of kiln. Downdraft kilns normally contain well-defined fireboxes where the massive buildup of flame goes on before the flame thrusts its heat up into the ware chamber. Updraft kilns usually have the area below the bottom ware shelf as the firebox, although there are exceptions to this arrangement. In both cases, the firebox takes the greatest beating during firing cycles, since it is subjected to thermal shock at the firing's onset. It must also withstand higher temperatures than the rest of the kiln because of its generating source and continuous flame impingement. Kilns made of bricks—whether they be refractory or insulating—constantly need repair in the firebox area because of these factors. The bricks here show considerable expansion and contraction compared to other parts of the kiln, and it is necessary to "beef up" this area if durability is desired. However, as already indicated in the introduction and as will be pointed out repeatedly in the following chapters, with kilns that use ceramic fibers as a hot face covering on the internal walls of the firebox, the material is unaffected by either thermal shock or flame impingement. Also, most of the characteristics of firebox abuse, such as expansion and contraction, are eliminated since the material does not expand. Ceramic fibers do

1–3 and 1–4. Gravity drip feed of oil is started with a paper fire in the retaining trough. Oil drips out of the orifice onto the paper fire, increasing heat under the cylinder casing. As the casing is heated, oil inside the cylinder vaporizes and builds up pressure which results in a forceful flame.

1–3.

Simple Oil Burner for Glass Furnace in Guadalajara—Side View

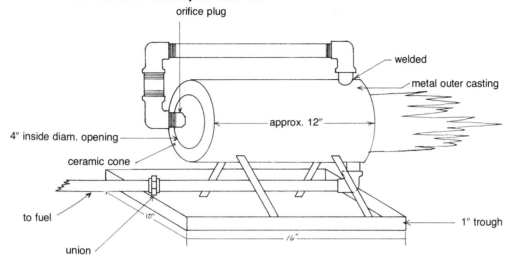

1–4.

Simple Oil Burner for Glass Furnace in Guadalajara—Front View

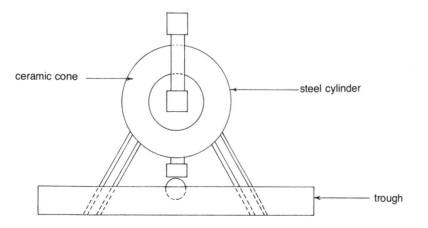

contract slightly (about 2 to 3 percent) if they are taken higher than their given hot-face working temperatures and therefore, if the internal surface of a kiln contains a ceramic-fiber face rated at 2,300°F. in the firebox area and heat generated during the firing exceeds this temperature, the material will shrink slightly and become somewhat brittle. It will not, however, expand again once it has contracted. One solution to the problem of slight contraction might be to use a higher-rated ceramic fiber in the firebox area, where working temperatures often reach 2,600°F. and higher. For example, some specialized ceramic fibers made of zircon have working temperatures as high as 4,500°F., but they are extremely expensive and not worth the cost since the lower-rated and more available alumina-silica fibers provide the same protection in the firebox area once they have contracted.

Natural gas is the cleanest of all natural fuels, followed by the liquid gases propane and butane and then the oils, such as No. 2 fuel oil, No. 1, and on down the line to crude oil and the solid fuels: coal, coke, and wood. Natural gas is lighter than air and therefore problems with burner carbonization rarely occur during the low preheat periods of kiln firings. Liquid gases, however, which are heavier than air, even when in a state of vaporization, often present carbonization problems during the preheat period unless the kiln is started at a high, rapid level of heat input. Orifices in liquified petroleum gas (LPG) burners are often too large to prevent some carbonization, both on the inside of the burner as well as in the firebox during the low heat prefiring cycles. This factor is all the more evident with oil burners, and one must be aware that carbon residue may be building up inside the burner itself, particularly on the inside nozzle end. The buildup can be very slight; however, after many firings, the carbon builds up sufficiently to actually constrict the opening of the burner. The result is the operation of a smaller burner than the one that was originally the proper size. Frequently this occurs with homemade burners which use the gas manifold as the burner mount; the orifice is in the manifold and the carbon can constrict the size of the orifice, thus cutting down substantially on the required B.t.u. input of heat to the kiln.

When carbonization takes place within the firebox itself—often directly in front of the burner—it is of little consequence to any of the functioning areas of the kiln or the burners because as the heat increases and the temperature becomes extreme (above 1,000°F.), all carboniza-tion, regardless of how thick, will burn off by the end of the firing cycle. One exception to this rule would be a kiln which has vertical burners situated directly under the burner port leading into the firebox—that is, a kiln where the firebox is a ceiling suspended directly over the burner. (Fig. 1–5.) If carbonization builds up substantially on the face of the firebox over the burner, heavy accumulated pieces of carbon can scale off and fall into the throat of the burner, causing a deflection of the flame and resulting in a very unsatisfactory flame shape entering the kiln. Once lodged into the throat of the burner during the early part of the firing cycle, the carbon refuse will not burn away since there is little heat generated within the burner itself. Fortunately, carbonization does not affect the new materials themselves since, as already mentioned, they are inert. Conventional materials such as insulating firebricks are organic, however, and therefore their insulating characteristics may be modified by heavy carbonization.

1–5.

Carbonization Accumulation

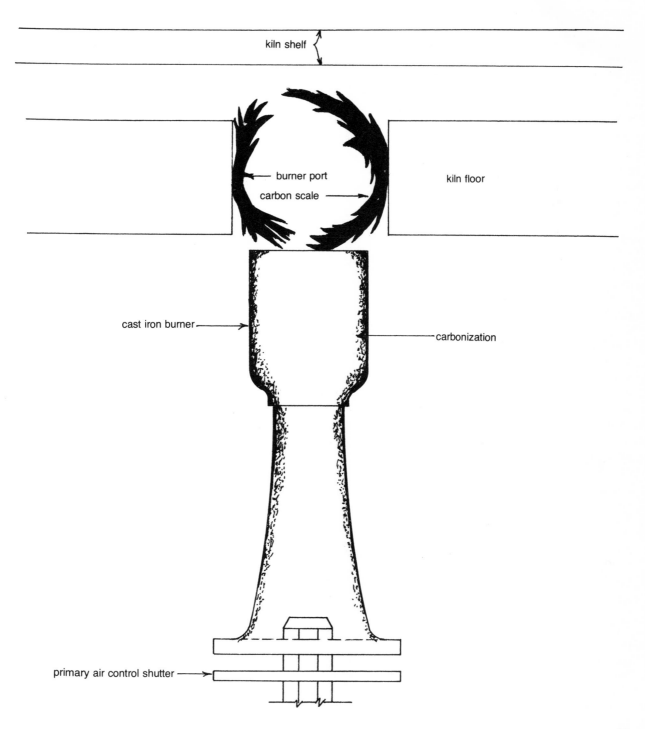

kiln shelf

burner port

carbon scale

kiln floor

cast iron burner

carbonization

primary air control shutter

2. *Updraft Catenary Kiln*

Updraft Catenary Kiln

The twelve-cubic-foot updraft catenary kiln discussed in this chapter is designed primarily for reduction firings to cone ten and is unique in that it chiefly depends on the utilization of an alumina-silica fiber blanket for its effectiveness. This blanket simplifies the kiln's construction and eliminates half the number of bricks needed. But the real value of the blanket lies in its thermal characteristics, as discussed in the introduction.

All specific measurements for the kiln are indicated in Figure 2–1. Refer to these measurements as you follow the instructions on construction.

Keep in mind that in the design of an updraft kiln, the kiln itself becomes the "stack," or chimney, which draws the heat and flame up through its interior and out of the top of the flue openings. The amount of heat and the type of reduction created are controlled by the dampers. Also noteworthy is the fact that the flame is directed *under the floor* (under the bottom shelf) from the sides of the kiln. This area—the firebox—helps to hold the heat of the flame longer in the kiln, thus generating better fuel efficiency. Because of the curvature of the catenary arch, the flame is set into a swirling motion on its passage up the wall. In this way, the flame bypasses the flue opening on its first turn and is driven into the pottery before escaping out of the top of the kiln.

Webster defines the word "catenary" as "The shape assumed by a perfectly flexible cord in equilibrium under given forces. The common catenary is exemplified in a chain or heavy cord hanging freely between two points of support."

The best structural shape of the catenary kiln is that in which the width equals the height of the arch. Since the arch acts as the roof and walls of the kiln combined, each brick thrusts its weight downward into the next supporting brick until the total weight of the structure rests on its foundation. Construction of the catenary kiln results in a form which is essentially self-supporting, requiring no buttresses, steel framing, tie rods, or buckstays. However, an optional steel frame of angle iron may be placed around the base of the kiln in order to prevent the arch from spreading after long usage.

Form Construction

First, determine the catenary kiln's curvature by hanging each end of a small linked chain on two supporting nails attached to the surface of a ½" sheet of plywood. The distance between the nails determines the width of the kiln at its base, and the apex of the chain's curvature will determine the interior height of the kiln. Carefully trace and cut out a template, following the curvature made by the hanging chain. Two templates are required to make the form on which the kiln will actually be built. Be certain that the templates are absolutely symmetrical; check this by superimposing one form against the other and then reverse them to see that they are identical. Then place the two templates parallel to one another at a distance equal to the desired length of the kiln. (Follow the *inside* measurements for Figure 2–1.) Connect these two end pieces with three horizontal 2" x 2" boards which are nailed *in-*

side the edges of the templates. (Fig. 2–2.) Do not allow these boards to project beyond the edges of the templates.

This frame is now covered with a ⅛″ sheet of masonite. If you encounter difficulty in bending the masonite over the narrow arch of the form, you can soak the material with water to make it flex more readily over the frame. When masonite is not available, thin wood slats may be used to cover the outside of the catenary frame. Once the form is completed and placed on the permanent kiln base, construction can begin.

2–1.
12-Cubic-Foot Updraft Kiln

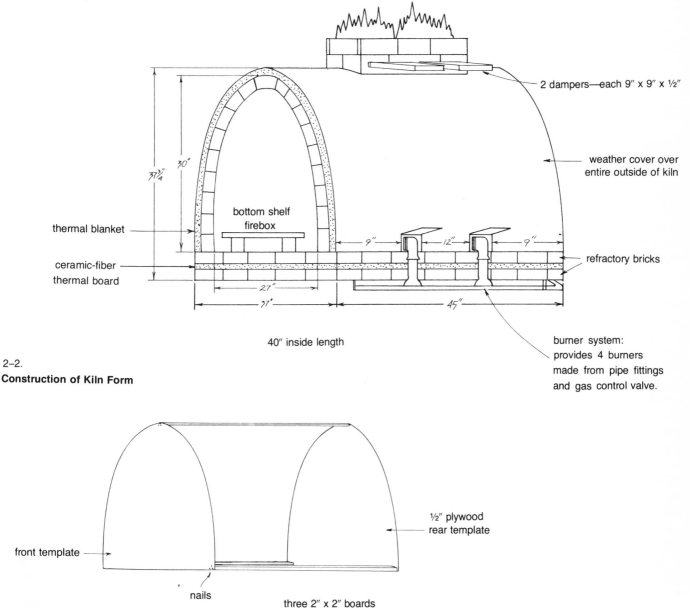

2–2.
Construction of Kiln Form

Kiln Base

Loading or unloading a small kiln at ground level is awkward, so it is preferable to have this kiln at waist height. The base may be constructed of concrete cinder building block reaching 32″ from ground level (the height of four 8″ blocks). A building block base is sufficiently stable to prevent shifting due to weather conditions or heat expansion from the kiln. A recommended though not essential procedure is to cement the blocks together for greater stability. The surface area on which the kiln will rest should measure 37″ x 45″, and be open (with the holes in the blocks turned upward) to allow heat to escape from the bottom of the kiln. (Fig. 2–3.) See that the entire base is level before constructing the refractory floor.

Kiln Floor

Before you place the form for the kiln on its base, a floor of refractory brick must first be constructed, measuring 37″ x 45″—the area for this kiln. Normally, two courses of brick are sufficient to serve as a heat insulator for the floor of the kiln. The bricks may be laid out on their wide side (the 4½″ side); together, the two courses will offer a refractory floor 5″ thick. For further floor insulation, place either ¼″-thick alumina-silica compressed board or a sheet of insulating thermal blanket in between the two brick courses. Mortar each brick in place with *fireclay*. (Mortar the consistency of heavy cream should be prepared before construction begins.) Dip each brick into fireclay slip, place it in position, and tap it with a masonry hammer to assure that it is well seated. The floor is the only portion of the kiln constructed with "hard" refractory brick, since it is the only area where movement of shelves, posts, and flame baffles takes place and the hard brick flooring will resist wear better than the soft insulating brick utilized in the remainder of the kiln. The refractory brick must have a thermal rating of 2600°F., comparable to that of the brick in the arch of the kiln.

Arch Form

After the kiln floor is completed, place the kiln arch form in position, allowing the floor to extend 5″ on all sides. (Fig. 2–4.) Small wooden blocks, not more than ½″ thick, should be placed under each corner of the kiln form. (Note the bottom of the form in Figs. 2–5 and 2–6.) These blocks will serve to "drop" the kiln form down from under the brick arch when the latter is completed so that the form will then be loose and can easily be pushed from under the arch. (See photo 2–8.)

Brick

The design of this kiln provides for an insulating firebrick, either K-26 Babcock and Wilcox or G-26 A.P. Green. This brick is rated at 2600°F. and has the characteristic of "reflecting" rather than "radiating" heat which must first be absorbed, as is the case with dense *refractory* brick. This thermal characteristic makes the kiln more economical to operate than one using refractory brick.

Blanket

Standard "straight" insulating firebricks (9″ x 4½″ x 2½″) are placed lengthwise against the kiln form to create a wall only 4½″ thick. (See Figs. 2–6 and 2–8.) Whereas normally, kilns are built with walls at least 9″ thick, in lieu of this, additional insulation for this catenary kiln is provided by an alumina-silica ceramic-fiber blanket. The material, which is only ½″ thick, is usually available in a roll 24″ wide by 24′ long, and the cost is based on a square foot charge, which is more economical than using additional bricks.

When you have covered the brick arch with a ceramic-fiber blanket, the material will not only help even out the temperature rise during firing, but will also help to retard cooling after the firing cycle is completed—a feature which virtually eliminates the most common cause of crazing in glazes. In addition, the blanket's thermal characteristics will cut by one third what the fuel cost would be for firing a kiln made only from refractory brick.

Burner Ports

Before you begin to construct the catenary kiln with insulating firebrick, it is important to indicate on the kiln form *where* the burner ports are to be. This kiln has two ports measured at an equal distance to one another on each side (see Fig. 2–1), which should be indicated on the side of the form with a pencil. If you will be using natural or liquid gas to fire the kiln, the ports may be 3″ square; if you use oil or other "heavy" fuels, they should be considerably larger. Now that the burner ports are indicated on the form, actual construction can begin.

Kiln Construction

Prepare two containers of fireclay as mortar for dipping bricks and for filling gaps. (One batch should be the consistency of heavy cream, the other a pliable consistency much like modeling clay.) The first brick course is cut at an angle to conform with the curvature of the form. Determine the angle by placing a straight brick at a right angle to the side of the form, then measuring the angle of the gap from the bottom of the brick to the surface of the kiln floor. With a pencil, rule off the angle of the gap on a sample brick and then cut with a standard wood-cutting handsaw. (You should acquire several cheap handsaws before starting this job.) This cut brick now serves as a template from which all other bricks on that row can be cut. As you place each brick against the kiln form, be certain that it has been dipped into the fireclay "slip" on all edges which will come in contact with the adjoining bricks in the course. When the initial two or three courses have been laid, you will have to make provision for the burner ports by either notching or piecing bricks in such a manner as to leave openings. (Note the wet mortar in Fig. 2–5 as well as the way in which the brick in the second course is notched to span the burner port.) In each course of bricks, the joints (where each brick butts against the next brick) are covered over by the next course in the standard masonry construction method. To assure that each joint is covered on each course, start every other row with a half rather than a full-length brick, so that each consecutive course covers the joints of the previous course. You can proceed by first laying one course of bricks on one side of the kiln form and then the next course along the opposite side, thus alternating courses as the walls of the arch grow together. At the beginning of each new course, butt a brick against the curvature of the kiln form to determine the angle of the cut.

Brick slivers may be used to fill gaps under bricks, so there is virtually no waste of materials. During wall construction, there will be occasions when several courses of brick will need no alteration of shape—most likely, halfway up the wall. Beyond this point the arch becomes more extreme and the angle more acute. Where angle gaps are too slight to be filled with a brick sliver, use heavy mortar to supplement. As you mortar each brick layer against the curvature of the kiln form, alignment may vary slightly from course to course, but even if a course does not actually press against the form during construction, this is not crucial since the form serves primarily as a guide. Only near the top must the brick rest on the form, because there it depends upon it for support.

2–3. Kiln base. Note that the holes in the blocks are turned upward to allow heat to escape from the bottom of the kiln.

2–4. The kiln floor extends 5″ beyond the sides of the arch form.

2–5. Provision is made for the burner ports by notching or piecing brick to leave openings.

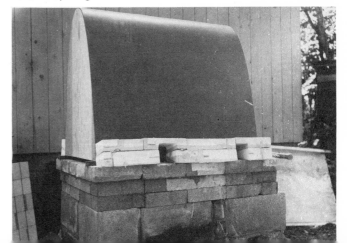

Keystone Brick

Continue building the walls until there is only an even gap directly over the top of the kiln form that cannot be filled in by laying a course of bricks as you have done up to this point. (Notice in Fig. 2–6 how the two walls at the top of the arch leave a gap directly down the middle of the form.) A "keystone" brick must now be shaped for inserting into this gap, and this brick will act as the main thrust-bearing brick after the kiln form has been removed. To determine the brick's shape, place a piece of cardboard flush against the face of the kiln where the gap is, and mark the angle of the gap with a pencil on the cardboard. The cardboard, cut at the angles marked, becomes a template for cutting the first keystone brick. Each keystone brick should fit absolutely snug against the adjoining walls at the top of the arch and be inserted *dry,* without mortar or slip. Bricks must be used broadside (across their width) in order to fill the gap properly. If there is a variance in the width of the gap across the top of the arch, you can check it by placing the cardboard template in position where the next brick is to be inserted. Whenever the angle varies from the original template, make another cardboard template which will fit properly before you cut another brick for that spot. In this final operation, precision is essential, since, as already mentioned, the keystone bricks are the load-bearing bricks which hold the entire arch in place. Since the total number of keystone bricks is no more than nine, it is better to make a template for each brick rather than have loose bricks which may eventually cause the kiln to become structurally unsound. During this finishing phase of construction, provision must be made for the flue openings in the kiln arch.

Flues

The flue openings are constructed in exactly the same manner as the burner ports: Openings are left in the arch. In the design for this kiln, flue openings are created at the top of the arch simply by omitting two groups of keystone bricks. (Fig. 2–7.) First, insert the facing keystone bricks in the front and rear of the arch and then brick in the remaining area beyond the flue openings until the arch is completed. Be certain that all keystone bricks are placed so as to support the bricks on both sides, as indicated in Fig. 2–7. This method of constructing flue openings is essentially the same one used for any type of masonry arch, whether roman, corbel, or beehive. After all of the keystone bricks are snugly and properly in place, the internal catenary form can be dropped by removing the small wooden blocks from under each corner and then pushed out. (Fig. 2–8 shows the form partially removed.) Although this may be done directly after the last keystone brick is in place, it is sometimes advisable to wait a day until the mortar in the bricks sets up.

Rear Wall and Kiln Wash

After the kiln form has been removed and the brick arch is free standing, you can proceed with construction on the rear wall. This wall can be built like a "plug" from inside the back of the arch or it can be butted up against the outside surface; the latter construction provides more space within the kiln for stacking of pottery. Dip the straight bricks in fireclay slip and lay one course upon another, each time overlapping the joints of the preceding course. Bricks protruding beyond the arch can be cut to conform to the curvature of the kiln. You can then incorporate the leftover pieces into the next course of bricks. The masonry portion of the kiln is now complete, except for the front door, which is literally bricked up. Now, using either a broad rough brush or a spatula, wash the outside facing of the entire kiln with a heavy fireclay slip in order to fill small crevices that were left open during construction. In some cases, it may be necessary to caulk exterior openings with heavy fireclay. (Note the exterior of the kiln walls in Fig. 2–8 compared to the interior.) The inside of the kiln is never caulked with slip or brushed with kiln wash above where the curvature of the arch leans over the stack area and is likely to drop particles of wash or caulking onto pot surfaces during firings.

Blanket

To apply the ceramic-fiber thermal blanket over the outside of the kiln, simply unroll the material over the arch (being careful not to fray it as you do so), and then cut off at the right length with a pair of scissors. (Fig. 2–9.) You can hold the blanket in place on the rear wall of the kiln by pinning it into the brick with roof nails. Any exposed areas of brick can be patched in with pieces of blanket cut to size. Remember to cut away pieces of blanket from the front of burner ports.

2–6. The "keystone" brick will be placed in the gap left at the top of the arch.

2–7.

Flue Openings

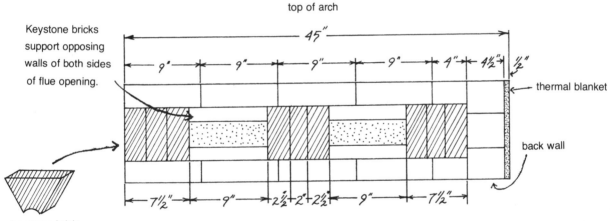

Keystone bricks support opposing walls of both sides of flue opening.

top of arch

45"

9" — 9" — 9" — 9" — 4" — 4½" — ½"

thermal blanket

back wall

7½" — 9" — 2½" 2" 2½" — 9" — 7½"

keystone brick

2–8. After the small wooden blocks have been removed, the dropped arch form can be pushed out.

2–9. Half of the ceramic-fiber thermal blanket has been placed on the completed brick arch.

Door and Dampers

The front door can be constructed with straight bricks shaped to fit the inward curvature of the kiln arch. Do *not* dip the bricks in slips: They remain dry since they are stacked and unstacked into position each time the kiln is fired. You should number the door bricks with some oxide so there will be no confusion as to where each brick is to be placed. (Note how in Fig. 2–10 the peepholes are indicated with a circle.) A few additional bricks can be placed around the flue openings in the top of the arch in order to build up a small stack. (See the top of the arch in Fig. 2–10; see also Fig. 2–11.) In order to control the flame through the adjustment of dampers, provide for two dampers to slide in and out over the flue openings, as shown in Figure 2–11. Make slits on one side of the stack in the same way openings were made for the burner ports. The damper shelves are 9″ x 9″ x ½″, and the best ones are made of silicon carbide, although mullite-based shelves also serve the purpose quite adequately. The two flue openings controlled by the dampers provide operational heat control of the kiln from front to rear. If the kiln is cooler in the front than the rear, the front damper is closed down to help hold heat in that area, and when the reverse situation occurs, the back damper can be closed down.

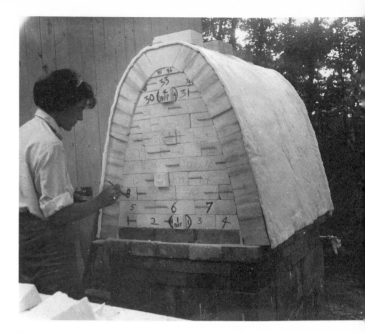

2–10. Peepholes are indicated with a circle and door bricks are numbered with a dark oxide slip.

2–11.

Side View of Stack

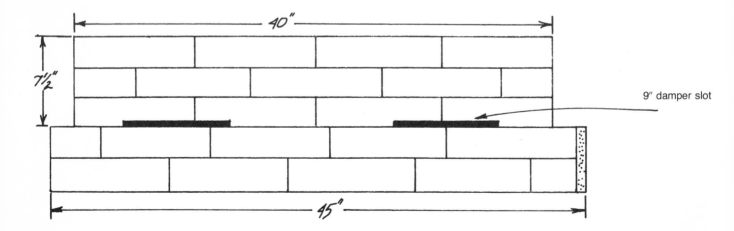

Weather Cover

Because of the extremely efficient thermal insulating characteristics of the materials used in this kiln, you don't have to build it inside a building or a room. Any protective weather covering can be placed over the outside surface to keep rain or snow from damaging the thermal blanket. A layer of white cement with a 1/3 ratio of cement to finishing sand is an effective covering. You can trowel the cement over a lath or hardware wire surface that has been laid down over the outside of the thermal blanket, and if you have tied down the wire over the arch and around the back end, it will help to serve as structural support to the kiln. Because of the properties of the thermal blanket, the firing of the kiln will not affect the cement covering outside. However, you should still "paint" two or three wash coats of cement of a very thin consistency over the first troweled coat a week or two after the kiln has been in use in order to help settle the final coating into place and create a finished appearance. Another more effortless cover is a 4' x 8' piece of galvanized sheet metal with a rectangular hole cut out of the center to allow for the protrusion of the stack. After notches have been cut on the bottom sides of the sheet metal cover so as to expose the burner ports, tie the sheet together across the bottom at the front and rear of the kiln with a length of stranded stainless cable. (Fig. 2–12.) You can cut an additional piece of sheet metal to the curvature of the rear of the kiln and insert it against the outside of the back wall, and then this back piece should be attached to the top covering by either using sheetmetal screws, tying with wire through holes, or clamping.

2–12. The completed arch is covered with a 4' x 8' piece of galvanized sheet metal.

Burner System

The burner system for this kiln is designed to accommodate four natural draft atmospheric burners made from pipe fittings. Although professional burners may certainly be used with the catenary kiln if you wish, the simple system that is described does not become maladjusted after long use as is sometimes the case with expensive and elaborate burners. This burner system is foolproof with natural or liquid gas and is simple to construct. As illustrated in Figures 2–13 and 2–14, the entire system is a "U"-shaped manifold made of pipe parts that is mounted on the kiln from the rear. The gas-controlling valve is located in the back of the kiln where the main fuel line is connected either to a bottled gas source or a natural gas meter. The manifold should first be assembled and placed into position around the kiln, and the exact locations of the orifice holes marked on the pipe just beneath the center of each burner port, so that when you install the system permanently, the burners will be directly centered in front of each burner port on the kiln.

2–14.
Burners

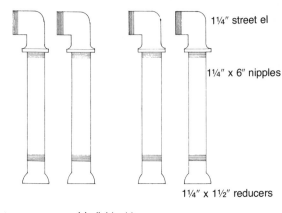

1¼" street el

1¼" x 6" nipples

1¼" x 1½" reducers

4 individual burners

Burners are spot welded over each orifice hole. They may also be clamped.

2–13.

Manifold System: Pipe Requirements for Burner System (on concrete block base)

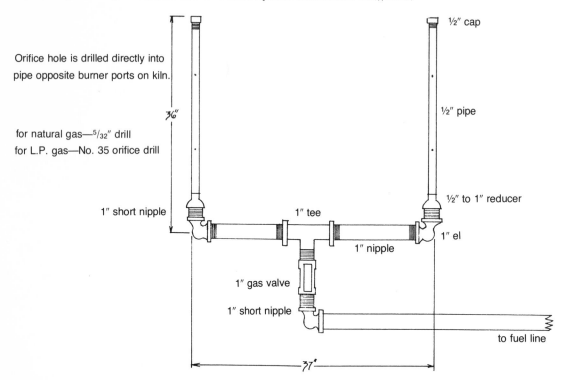

Orifice hole is drilled directly into pipe opposite burner ports on kiln.

for natural gas—⁵/₃₂" drill
for L.P. gas—No. 35 orifice drill

½" cap

½" pipe

½" to 1" reducer

1" el

1" short nipple

1" tee

1" nipple

36"

1" gas valve

1" short nipple

to fuel line

37"

B.T.U.

For firing to cone ten, 360,000 B.t.u. are required. If you use natural gas as fuel, you will need a $^5/_{32}''$ drill to make the orifice hole for each burner. Each burner will then provide sufficient B.t.u. to fire twelve cubic feet of kiln space. With liquid petroleum gas, a No. 35 $^7/_{64}''$ orifice drill will allow the correct B.t.u. for each burner to fire the kiln.

First, choose the correct orifice hole suited to the type of fuel you will use—natural gas or propane. Then mark and drill the correct hole directly into the manifold pipe. Place the manifold on the kiln, and mount the individual burners over the orifices by means of spot welding or clamping. When the entire system is finished, the street-elbow portion of the burners should project about one inch into the kiln.

Flame

The size relationship between the manifold pipe where the burner is mounted and the opening at the bottom of each burner provides the proper "primary" air ratio which will be drawn up into the burner when ignition takes place. The burner flame should be rather long and yellow with a small blue cone appearing near the front of the burner nozzle. The primary air being drawn up into the burner will cause a venturi effect that will increase the velocity of the flame on the tip of the burner and make a soft reverberating sound. Light the burner system with caution. First open the gas valve slightly and insert a lit match (use long fireplace matches) under the bottom of each burner at the orifice opening. If a flame does not appear when the orifice is ignited, insert the match at the burner nozzle.

As mentioned before, burners using heavy fuels can also be used on this kiln; it is a matter of personal preference or need. But oil burners, because of the density of the fuel, sometimes require a blower system and are therefore more complicated to construct and operate.

Firebox

The bottom shelf for stacking pottery ware should be a minimum of 4" off the floor of the kiln. It is the area under this shelf that is used as the "firebox" and where most of the flame is directed. The total space above this firebox area acts as the "stack" which creates the draft that carries the flame up and out of the flue opening on top. As noted in chapter 1, this is basically the way an updraft kiln functions.

Stacking Area

The stacking area, the space within the kiln which will contain the ware during firing, constitutes the interior space above the firebox. Due to the narrowing arch, the stacking area becomes more restricted toward the top of the kiln. Therefore, when arranging both shelves and pottery, compensation must be made to allow free circulation of the flame through the increasingly restricted space. (The measurements in Figure 2–5 show the narrowing stacking area.)

2–15.

Inside Stacking Area

front view

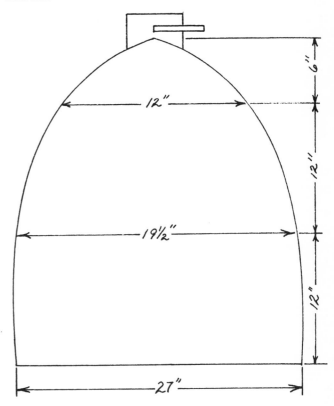

Heat Saturation

This kiln was specifically designed with four burners—two on each side—in order to develop even heat saturation during the firing cycle. Evenness of the heat is controlled through flame baffling at each burner port. On each side of the kiln, the flame of one burner should be directed vertically up the inside wall by means of a small flat baffle brick 2½" high placed about 3" away from the inside wall of the kiln and facing the burner port. (Fig. 2–16.) The flame of the other burner on the same wall should be directed horizontally across the floor of the kiln. Instead of a flat baffle brick, place a wedge-shaped one in the same location in front of the burner port, where it will act to split the flame as it enters the kiln and direct it into the firebox area. The same thing is done with the flame on the opposite side of the kiln. (Fig. 2–17.) The result will be that a flame directed up the inside wall of the kiln will be opposite from a flame directed across the floor, and vice versa.

Flame

Because the catenary arch is completely a curvature from floor to ceiling, the direction of the flame from the burner ports follows the configuration of the arch. During early firing periods it is often possible to look through a peephole and see the flame sweep up the inside wall of the arch, bypass the flue openings, circulate through the ware on the shelves, and then drive straight up out of the flue. With reduction firing, this pattern becomes a definite asset, since the flame is held in the kiln a little longer. The length of time the flame stays in the kiln contributes toward using fuel at its maximum efficiency and also results in effective reduction firing.

2–16.

Heat Saturation—Front View

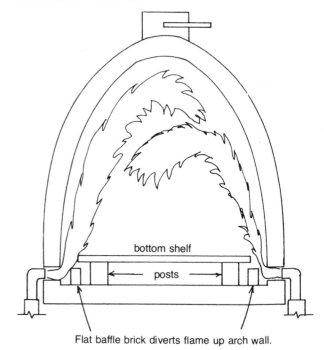

bottom shelf

posts

Flat baffle brick diverts flame up arch wall.

2–17.

Heat Saturation—Top View

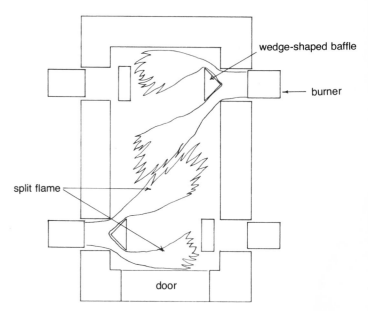

wedge-shaped baffle

burner

split flame

door

Conclusion

The configuration and construction of the catenary kiln allow for the expansion and contraction which inevitably occur during firing cycles. While each brick on the catenary directs all of its thrust into the supporting brick underneath, the expansion of the rising heat literally moves the kiln up and out during the firing. When the kiln cools, the entire kiln contracts and each brick settles back into place. If, over a period of several years' use, interior wall bricks leave gaps from expansion, the exterior thermal-blanket covering will hold in heat and not allow the kiln to become less efficient.

The structure of the catenary kiln is such that it can be converted from an updraft to a downdraft kiln. (See ch. 7, Fig. 7–6.) Furthermore, it can also have a "piggyback" kiln attached to the end, providing both an updraft and a downdraft kiln within the same structure. This system utilizes the fuel from one kiln to fire the secondary kiln. When two catenary kilns are built back to back, the kilns share the same back wall: When one kiln is fired to glaze temperatures, the other can simultaneously be bisque fired by using the "waste" fuel of the glaze firing.

Materials List for the Twelve-Cubic-Foot Updraft Catenary Kiln

Kiln base:
45 concrete cinder blocks (each 8″ x 8″ x 16″)
(Construction may be a combination of partial block and concrete poured base as illustrated in Fig. 2–3.)

Catenary arch form:
One 4′ x 8′ sheet of ⅛″ nontempered Masonite
One 4′ x 4′ sheet of ½″ exterior plywood
Three 2″ x 2″ pine wood boards, each 39″ long

Bricks:
250 insulating (standard straights—9″ x 4½″ x 2½″)
90 hard refractory (standard straights—each 9″ x 4½″ x 2½″)

Mortar:
100-lb bag of fireclay

Ceramic fiber blanket:
50 sq. ft. alumina-silica, ½″ thick, 6 lb. density

Damper shelves:
2 (silica-carbide or mullite, each 9″ x 9″ x ½″)

Burner parts (see Figs. 2–13 and 2–14):
2 pieces ½″ galvanized pipe with threads on both ends, each 33″ long
2 pieces galvanized nipples
2 pieces galvanized elbows
5 pieces 1″ galvanized short nipples
2 pieces 1″ to ½″ galvanized reducers
1 piece 1″ galvanized tee
One 1″ gas valve
One roll plumbers strapping with holes (for hanging burners)
4 pieces 1¼″ x 6″ galvanized nipples
4 pieces 1¼″ galvanized street elbows
4 pieces 1¼″ x 1½″ galvanized reducers

Weather cover:
100-lb. bag powdered white cement
100-lb bag finishing sand
2¼ pieces lath wire (standard size 2′ x 8′ apiece; hardware or chicken wire may be substituted)
1 roll bailing wire (for tying lath wire to kiln)
1 lb. roofing nails (wide head for pinning wire down)

3. Downdraft Roman-Arch Kiln

The twenty-cubic-foot kiln discussed in this chapter is in essence a sprung-arch kiln which is sometimes referred to as a "segmented arch," although it is commonly recognized as being a Roman arch in structure. Serving a somewhat different purpose than the catenary form, this kiln combines the features of a rectangular stacking space constructed with insulating brick, plus a ½"-thick thermal ceramic-fiber board, and ceramic-fiber liquid cement. Because of its superior insulating qualities, the kiln reaches cone ten easily and retains heat extremely well during the cooling cycle after temperature has been reached.

Figures 3–1 through 3–4 show all specific measurements for construction using standard 9" straight insulating bricks rated at 2,600°F. However, with the application of a ceramic-fiber thermal blanket and board, nearly 50 percent of the brick that would normally be needed for insulating and structural purposes is eliminated. The width of the walls is only 4½" compared to the minimum 9"-wall required when no blanket is used. The thermal blanket and the board—which is laid under the kiln floor—replace additional bricks by acting as a heat barrier beyond the exterior face of the bricks. While the insulating bricks provide a means of soaking up heat at the height of the firing cycle, the backup blanket feeds back a greater amount of the brick heat into the kiln chamber. Because of this effect, heat can continue to rise after cone ten has been reached and the kiln closed down. Since it is not unusual to find cone 11 down even though the kiln was shut off at the maturity of cone 10, experience in firing this kiln often requires a shutting off at cone 9 in order to reach cone 10, unless a soaking period is initiated. If soaking is a part of your objective in firing, then you should be cautious because of the heat acceleration after shut-off. Soaking would require a cutting back of B.t.u. input from the burners in order to equalize the heat. Consumption of fuel is extremely efficient and economical with this kiln; it will consume only 16 to 20 feet of natural gas compared to three times that amount for conventional kilns without ceramic-fiber materials. After several years of usage, gas consumption will rise slightly to 18 to 21 cubic feet of natural gas, provided all firing conditions remain in control.

The ceramic-fiber materials completely cover all brick joints, thus preventing substantial heat loss, even through expansion joints. The resulting superior heat buildup, however, also makes for superior heat retention after the kiln has been shut down. Therefore, a normal firing cycle requiring 8 hours to bring down cone ten also requires not less than 20 hours for the cooling cycle to be completed so that the kiln may be opened.

The primary purpose of this downdraft kiln is to bring about a superior firing result by the marriage between a conventional structure of insulating firebrick and supplemental new materials, thorough heat circulation within the kiln for the best effect on the ware, and by providing a stacking space that will allow pots to be placed on all levels without restriction, from the bottom to the top of the kiln.

Top View

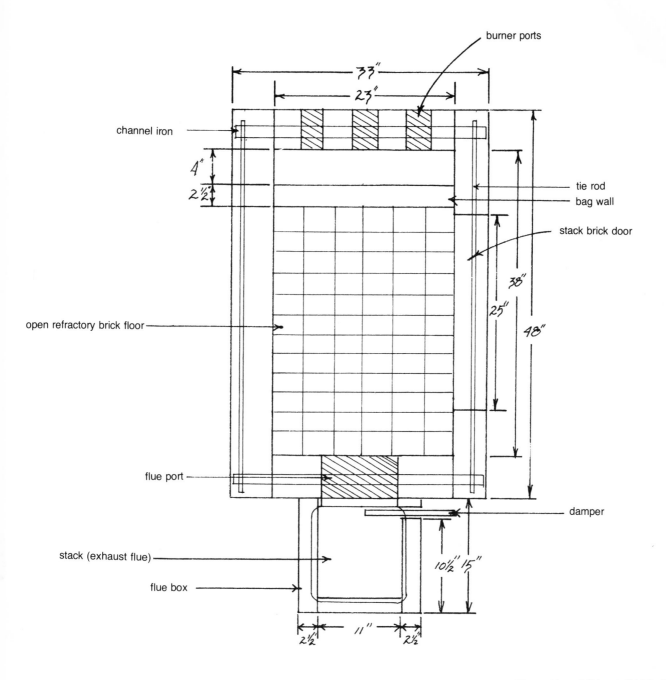

burner ports

channel iron

33″

23″

tie rod
bag wall

stack brick door

4″

2½″

open refractory brick floor

38″

25″

48″

flue port

damper

stack (exhaust flue)

flue box

10½″ 15″

11″

2½″ 2½″

Channel iron: 33″ long, 4″ high, 3/16″ wide

Tie rod: 45″ long, ½″ diam., ½″ nut with 1″ thread

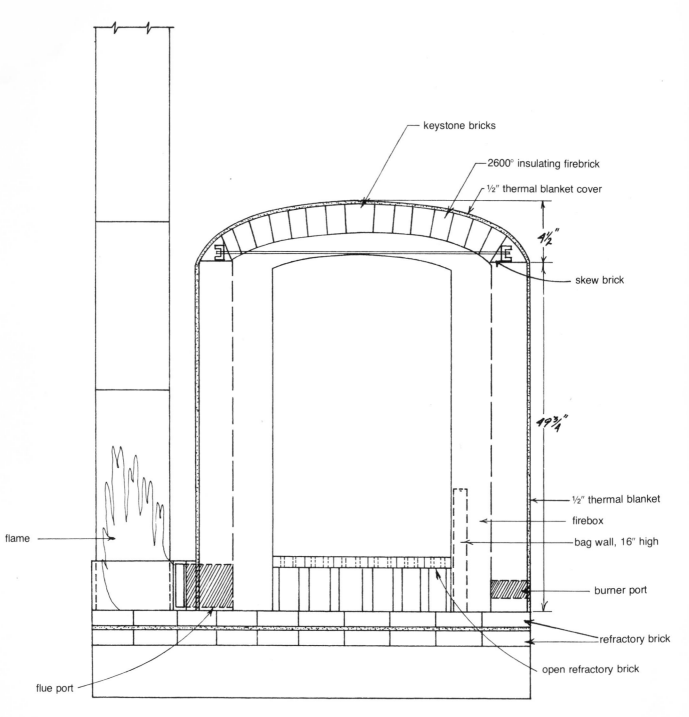

keystone bricks

2600° insulating firebrick

½″ thermal blanket cover

4½″

skew brick

19¾″

½″ thermal blanket

firebox

bag wall, 16″ high

burner port

refractory brick

open refractory brick

flame

flue port

3–3.

Side View—Burner Side

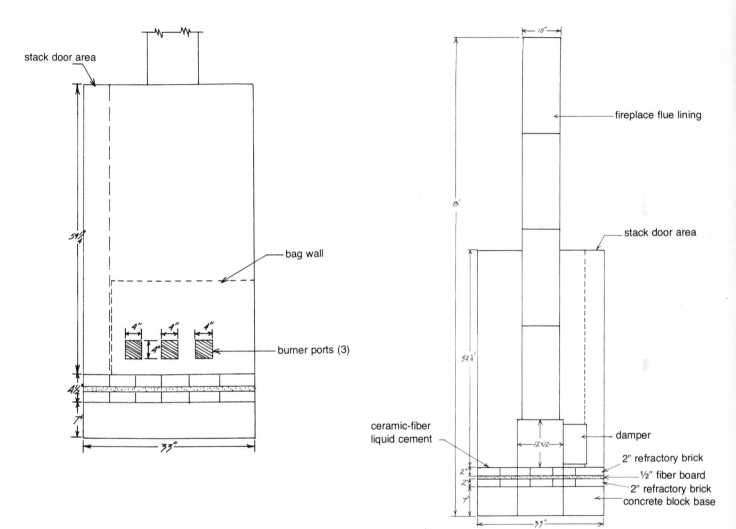

3–4.

Side View—Stack Side

Foundation

In order to simplify stacking operations, this kiln should be elevated a bit off ground level; the surface area needed is 45½" x 29". For the foundation, place 16 concrete cinder building blocks at ground level to form an area 48" x 38", less the flue stack area. Lay the cinder blocks down with the holes turned upward. (Fig. 3–5.) You can cement this group of blocks together, but it is not essential to do so. However, the foundation must be absolutely level.

Kiln Floor

A hard refractory brick surface is mortared over the concrete cinder blocks. Since the important thing is to have a firm, solid floor upon which the kiln shelves, posts, and ware will eventually be placed, you can use any size hard bricks so long as they are high-temperature material. (In Figure 3–7 a 12" x 12" x 2½" flat brick is being used rather than the standard 9" x 4" x 2½" straight brick.) Mortar each brick into place with fireclay the consistency of heavy cream.

Using a broad cold chisel and a hammer, you can hand cut refractory bricks to fit a specified area. There is no need of incurring the expense or time to have the brick cut with a power saw. Tap continuously along a scored line of separation against the brick, first on one side and then on the other. After this line has been scribed with moderate chisel blows, break the brick along the desired line by means of a strong thrusting blow. (Fig. 3–6.)

When the first layer of hard brick has been placed in position and mortared, install a layer of ½" compressed ceramic-fiber board. (Fig. 3–7.) No need to glue the board down with a mortar slip, since the board has a compressed rigidity. Because it is not hard like refractory brick, it may be cut to size with a sharp knife or Stanley cutting blade. After the foundation has been completely fitted with ceramic-fiber board, place another layer of hard brick down and mortar it in place to complete the surface which will eventually be exposed to the heat of the firebox. (Fig. 3–8.) The ceramic-fiber board underneath becomes a heat-barrier insulation which protects the lower concrete foundation, and it also helps the upper layer of bricks to reflect heat back up into the kiln. The total thickness of the kiln floor above the concrete foundation is now 5½".

3–5. The cinder blocks are laid with the holes turned up to allow heat penetration.

3–6. A strong thrusting blow with a cold chisel cleanly cuts refractory brick.

3–7. Ceramic-fiber board is placed on top of the refractory brick floor.

3–8. The ceramic-fiber board is sandwiched between two layers of refractory brick to form the floor insulation.

Brick Construction

This kiln utilizes the same insulating firebrick as does the twelve-cubic-foot catenary kiln: a K-26 Babcock and Wilcox or G-26 A.P. Green. (See ch. 2 for the characteristics of this reflective brick.)

The first two courses of bricks are laid down with slip and mortar around the outside perimeter of the kiln floor. The brick seams (where each brick butts up against the next) always overlap the seams of the brick on the adjacent course below. This standard masonry technique assures a locking action when bricks overlap, thus helping to prevent walls breaking straight down a seam line. Leave a 10¾″ gap open on the small jutting platform of the kiln floor for the flue opening area. (Fig. 3–9.) Upon laying down the fourth course, narrow the gap to 8½″, and upon the fifth course the gap is bridged completely. During the brick laying operation, use a level constantly to check that the alignment of each course stays true with the previous course. Also, leave every second or third brick in a course slightly ajar (not butted up to the next brick) in order to provide expansion joints in the wall.

3–9. A gap is left open on a small jutting platform of the kiln floor for the flue.

37

Burner Ports

Since this kiln is designed for either natural or liquid gas fuel, the burner ports should be 4″ square. If you use an oil burner system instead, increase the size of the ports by about 25 percent.

After you have laid down the first two courses of insulating brick upon the kiln floor, the area for the burner ports must be clearly drawn with a carpenter's hard lead pencil. Indicate the position for the three burner port openings—each to measure four square inches—directly opposite the flue opening. On the next two courses (courses 3 and 4), notch the course to conform to the marked area. On the fourth course, the bricks are notched in such a manner as to span the top of the ports. (Fig. 3–10.)

With the completion of the fourth course of bricks, the firebox and ware stack areas become well defined. These areas, which measure 38″ x 23″, will contain the heat-generating source for the rest of the kiln. The arrangement of bricks within this space constitutes the inside floor for the kiln, and will be discussed later.

Walls

From the fourth course on, continue to build the walls of the kiln up, course upon course, until you have completed a total of 15 additional courses. During this portion of construction, leave a 25-inch gap as an opening for the door at right angles to the flue and burner ports. This will be the front of the kiln. (Fig. 3–11.) Remember to continue to overlap each seam with the course below throughout the entire construction. Use a whole brick at the beginning of each alternate course and a half brick at the start of every other course in order to get the overlapping of seams.

Arch Form Templates

After the walls have been completed, the wooden arch form must be set up. Use two pieces of wood measuring 37¾″ long by 5″ wide and ¾″ thick to constitute the two arch form templates upon which the kiln brick arch will be built. Cut these templates by marking the center point—15⅞″ from the end—and scribing an arc from the bottom corner at one end, through the center mark at the top, and back to the bottom corner at the opposite end. (See Fig. 3–20 for an illustration of the arch form template.) Make two identical arch-form board templates.

Next, make 18 wooden slats measuring 23″ long by 1½″ wide to provide the support for the arch bricks as they

3–10. The fourth course of bricks is notched so as to span the top of the burner ports.

3–11. A 25″-opening is left as the door entrance of the kiln.

are laid up across the top of the kiln. Although the illustrations show a ¾″-thick slat, the thickness of the slats is not crucial.

The wooden arch forms are supported in a relatively simple way. Two boards measuring 37½″ by 4″ act as supporting horizontal cross members directly under the arch form templates. These arch form boards must fit just inside the kiln walls at the top course of the wall bricks. Cut four additional boards to use as upright supports underneath the horizontal cross boards. (Fig. 3–12.) These boards can be any width and thickness, so long as they are sufficiently long to place the curved arch-form template boards within ¾″ of the top face of the last course of wall bricks. The entire assembly of boards, when placed inside the kiln, is mainly supported by gravity. First, place the four vertical upright boards in each inside corner of the kiln; next, the horizontal cross member boards are placed atop the vertical uprights; and, lastly, place the two curved arch-form board templates which have been tacked together at the center top with two nails upon the supporting cross-member boards. The one slat tacked with two small headless nails on top of the arch-form board templates will prevent these boards from tilting over and falling on their side during the brick lay-up operation. (Fig. 3–13.) The curved arch-form boards should be so situated that once a slat is placed under the first course of bricks, the outside edge of the brick will be no lower than the top of the last course of wall bricks. (Fig. 3–14.)

3–13. The center slat is tacked onto the two arch forms to hold the boards in place during brick lay-up.

3–14. The outside edge of the first course of arch bricks is no lower than the top surface of the wall bricks.

3–12. Boards are placed upright in the corners to support the arch form.

Skew Brick and Thrust Support

The skew brick is the load-bearing brick which takes the thrust from the completed arch, and must be cut at an angle conforming with the angle of the first course of arch bricks as it rests upon the curved arch form. To determine this angle, place the brick on the end of the curved arch form at the kiln's inside end wall; then put another standard straight brick in front of the arch brick so that the angle of the arch brick can be traced upon the end of the other brick. This line will show the exact angle at which each of the skew bricks needs to be cut. (See Fig. 3–14.) After you have cut two and one-half skew bricks for each end of the arch, on both sides place a piece of steel channel iron measuring 33″ x 4″ directly behind the skew brick with the iron's flat face flush against the back of the skews. (Fig. 3–15.) Each channel iron has two ½″ holes, one inch from each end, in which a tie rod is placed to hold the two steel channel irons in check. The tie rods, which are 45″ long and ½″ in diameter, have a threaded end that provide for a washer and nut to be placed on the rod outside the channel irons. Set the skew brick and the channel iron in position on top of the last course of wall bricks *before* you actually begin constructing the arch. Make certain that the bottom edge of the skew brick is flush with the inside of the kiln wall before you tighten the tie-rod nuts. Always make this adjustment by hand, not with a wrench.

3–15. The channel iron support goes flush up against the back of the skew brick.

Arch Construction

The arch is constructed by laying up alternating courses of insulating brick from skew-brick face on one side to skew-brick face on the opposite side. That is, after you have laid up a course of bricks on one side with mortar and slip, you then lay up the next course on the opposite side until a total of seven courses have been completed on each side. This will leave a center gap, where you insert the keystone brick that will carry the thrust once the wooden arch form has been removed. (Fig. 3–16.) Before laying up each course, place a separate wooden slat across the top of the arch forms to support that course. No other means of securing the slat to the arch form is necessary than the weight of the bricks during lay-up.

You are now ready to put in the keystone brick. To find the right size for the keystone brick, place a piece of cardboard flush against the face of the adjacent arch brick and mark the exact angle of the keystone gap on the cardboard. Then cut the cardboard with a pair of scissors to create a template with the right angle for the cutting of the keystone brick. Using the cardboard template as a guide, cut a new brick across its face (broadside). Each keystone brick must fit absolutely snug against the adjoining walls at the top of the arch, and each of these ten keystone bricks should be inserted dry, without mortar or slip. If there is a variance in the width of the gap across the top of the arch, you can check it by placing the template in position where the next brick will be inserted. When the angle varies from the original template, cut another cardboard template that will fit properly before cutting the keystone brick for that position. In placing keystone bricks, it is best first to seat the front brick and then the rear one, alternating from front to back until the last place to be filled is the very center of the arch. Figure 3–17 shows how each keystone brick is tapped into place with a wood block and a hammer. After all keystone bricks are in, another longer wood block, which spans all keystone bricks at once, can be placed on top and gently tapped together in order to produce a uniform thrust and seating of the bricks. (Figs. 3–18 and 3–19.) Now the arch can be "sprung"—that is, the supporting wooden forms removed, at which point the brick arch "seats itself" by dropping its weight up tightly against the supporting skew bricks and channel iron. (Figs. 3–20 and 3–21.) Remove the supporting wooden arch forms by simply knocking out the vertical upright boards inside the kiln. Everything will immediately come falling in, except the brick arch, and you will experience the moment of truth.

The width of the arch measures 23″ from the inside wall at the rear of the kiln to the front. Do not extend the arch beyond this point, for that would only prevent the continuation of the back and front walls from covering the gap created by the rise in the arch.

3–16. The space in the center of the arch is for the keystone brick.

3–17. Tap each keystone brick into place with a block and hammer.

3–18. Note the placement of the keystone brick before seating.

3–19. After the keystone brick has been seated, it is flush with the top of the arch.

3–20. The wooden arch form is knocked out with a hammer.

3–21. The thrust of the arch is carried by the steel channel iron braced on the outside of the skew brick.

The Door Arch

Now that the main arch is complete, the top opening of the door must be spanned. Using one board measuring 25″ long by 4″ wide, determine the curve and cut it in the same way you did the main-arch wooden forms. Place the board at the top of the door opening with two supporting uprights, and lay up one course of bricks by the short width (2½″ wide) as was done for the arch construction. However, don't use any slots on top of the door arch board. An alternative to spanning the door opening is simply to insert a steel rod through a series of bricks, which, when placed across the top of the door opening, become a continuation of the front wall up to the top of the main arch.

The rear wall of the kiln is then continued until it reaches the point where it is flush with the top of the main arch span.

Thermal Blanket

Covering the kiln with a ceramic-fiber blanket becomes a simple upholstery task. You can cut the blanket to size with a pair of scissors and then place it in position on the outside of the kiln. During application, hold it in place with large head roofing nails gently tapped through the blanket and anchored into the body of the insulating brick behind. (See the description of this operation in ch. 2.)

Weather Covering

Because the thermal blanket is vulnerable to abuse from pelting rain and other weather conditions, it should be protected by covering that can be maintained in good condition. Construction lath wire covering the entire kiln like a skin is the best way both to protect the blanket and to provide added support for the overall kiln structure. Galvanized lath wire is best because it will not rust. Anchor the lath wire over the kiln with masonry nails, which you drive through the wire into the cement cinder block foundation below. Use pieces of bailing wire to tie areas of lath wire together and create the continuous skin over the kiln. By anchoring the lath wire down on one side of the kiln and then pulling it taut up over the arch and down the other side, you can give substantial strength to its placement upon the kiln. For stability, nail the wire down into the concrete block on both sides of the kiln. Additional pieces of lath wire can then be attached with bailing wire at the top front and rear, and then pulled down in the same manner to be attached to the foundation. Wear working gloves since you can easily cut your hands handling the lath wire. If lath construction wire is not available, you can use hardware, or even chicken wire, just as efficiently.

Next, make a mixture of white cement and sand into a trowling consistency of 3/1 sand to white cement and cover the entire surface of the wire with it. (Fig. 3–22.) This first cement application must be completely cured before you apply another coating. The next coating, however, is a wash consistency at a ratio of 1/1 cement to sand. Painted on top of the first coat with a paper hanging brush, this second coating creates a clean, smooth finish which further seals the pores of the first coat and improves weather conditioning.

The Door

The door is made up of individual insulating bricks cut and fitted to conform to the door opening. During the fitting operation, provide for a peephole every few courses so that you can see pyrometric cones during the firing cycle; simply leave a 3″ gap in the center of a door brick. Calculate the position of a spy hole at a level that will coincide with a shelf within the kiln. Each brick is fitted dry, without slip or mortar, since the door is stacked or unstacked each time the kiln is loaded or unloaded. Number each brick with an oxide slip so that you have the right order when you are ready to stack the door. (Fig. 3–22.)

3–22. Lath wire and a covering of white cement and sand provide a weather cover for the kiln.

Stack and Damper

After the kiln is finished, the damper and stack can be put together. Note in Figures 3–1, 3–2, and 3–4 that a refractory brick support must be constructed that provides both a slot for the damper shelf as well as a supporting base for the clay flue liner, which is then stacked on top of this base. The refractory base must be set flush against the flue opening in such a way as to prevent heat from escaping between the stack and the outside wall of the kiln during operation. Although Figure 3–23 shows 12″ x 12″ refractory slabs being used for the supporting section of the stack, 9″ straight bricks can be used just as effectively.

This section completed—including the damper slot—now mount four 12″ clay flue liners, each 2′ long, one on top of the other so they reach a total height of 8′. Place four pieces of 1½″ x 1½″ x ⅛″ angle irons at each outside corner of the stack as vertical supporting devices. Plumbers strapping—a coil of galvanized metal with ¼″ holes—is then wrapped around the entire circumference of the stack and angle irons and bolted tightly together. (Figs. 3–24 and 3–25.)

During the first few firings of the kiln, the heat escaping through the flue and up into the stack will often cause the clay flue liners to crack. (See Fig. 3–25.) Since the clay flue-liner body is tight and brittle, the heat passing through it will make the liner develop its own expansion joints, but once this initial action has occurred, further cracks rarely appear. The flue liners supported by the outer straps will now expand and contract slightly every time the kiln is fired. If you want the liner to be insulated, you can line the inside with a layer of ceramic-fiber blanket. You can glue the blanket to the inside with an application of sodium-silicate solution, but be careful since the blanket may eventually become brittle after excessive heat passage from the lower areas of the flue—this area is essentially an extention of the firebox, where temperatures exceed 2,300°F.—and it will begin to flake off in large pieces and fall down and choke the flue opening. Keep in mind that the purpose of the flue is simply to create a draft out of the bottom of the kiln and pass heat and flame out and upward outside the kiln; it need not also retain heat as does the kiln itself. Since this is the principal function of the stack, you could use a circular metal stack instead of clay flue liners, except that the metal stack is less available and more costly.

3–23. 12″ x 12″ refractory bricks support the bottom of the stack.

3–24. Plumbers strapping and angle iron hold the four fireplace liners in position.

3–25. A long 3″ x ¼″ bolt is drawn through the plumbers strapping.

The damper is nothing more than a piece of kiln shelf measuring 10½" x 16" x 1" (the thickness of this shelf is not crucial since it will not carry any weight) which opens and closes the flue opening during kiln operation. At the time you are constructing the supporting section of the stack with a slot to allow passage of the damper shelf, you can calculate the slot so it fits a shelf already on hand.

The damper shelf must actually be longer than the area in which it goes, in order to facilitate grasping and positioning it. You should place the damper in various positions in the flue openings and mark these positions on the outside of the shelf so as to have a visual guide for its insertion during operation. (See Fig. 3–23.) A straight line made with a dark oxide slip across the damper indicating ½, ¼, ⅓, ⅔ open positions should serve the purpose. The best time to mark the damper is before the inside kiln floor has been put in place so that you can easily see it from the inside of the kiln through the flue opening.

Interior Floor

The interior floor is a necessary secondary floor within the kiln which provides a space through which the flame may travel without obstruction during its exit through the flue. If it is removed for any reason and pottery is placed in this area, immediate detrimental changes in flame circulation will occur. (See ch. 9 on trouble shooting.)

The remaining space in the bottom of the kiln, between the outside of the firebox and the inside wall of the flue opening, is reserved for placement of the interior floor. Again, all of the bricks in this area are hard refractory bricks with no mortar or slip of any sort. However, before installation, you can paint the inside of the kiln floor bed and surrounding surfaces, as far up as the bottom of the door opening, with a coating of ceramic-fiber liquid cement for further protection from flame abuse and intense heat. Place straight 9" refractory bricks upright in a pattern over the kiln floor so as to allow ample flame circulation to the flue opening. On top of these upright supporting bricks, place the false floor bricks, all of which have holes through them. If such bricks are not available, standard 9" refractory bricks can be used and placed about one inch apart from one another to allow flame passage. Bridge the floor bricks from supporting brick to supporting brick until you have completely covered the entire floor stack area. (Fig. 3–26.) The top of the interior floor is normally level with the bottom of the door opening. From this level upward, you can put in the posting and shelves for stacking,

taking care to place shelf posts wherever underlying upright supporting bricks are located under the interior floor. If a post goes elsewhere, the weight of all the ware and shelves may cave in the interior floor later and result in a stack collapse during the firing cycle. Such excessive heat is generated under the interior floor that undue pressure from above can considerably weaken the bricks laid in at that location.

Firebox and Bag Wall

The bag wall, which functions as a fire wall, is placed inside the kiln from front to back, four inches in front of the burner ports. The space between the inside wall of the kiln and the bag wall is the firebox—the heat-generating source for the entire kiln. Put the bag wall in *dry,* without any mortar; use hard refractory bricks since the wall receives direct flame impingement. (See Fig. 3–2.) The suggested height of the bag wall is 16" when first placed into the kiln. In addition to being a part of the firebox retention area, the bag wall primarily determines how the heat from the burners will be thrust into the kiln and through the ware: If the bag wall is too low, the kiln will fire hot in the bottom and cool at the top, and if it is too high, the kiln will fire hot on top and cool in the bottom. You can only determine the right height for even heat throughout after several firings of the kiln. The height suggested is based on experience in attaining the best heat circulation, but it should be understood that adjustment may be necessary. Chinks opened in the face of the bag wall can allow heat to reach a compromise saturation which will benefit the control of heat during a firing cycle. For this reason the bag wall is inserted dry, so that adjustment may be made without the agony of undoing mortared and fixed settings. The bag wall and the firebox work together to create the consistency and control in the firing system of this kiln.

Burner System

Figure 3–27 clearly shows a system designed and suited for temperatures in the stoneware range and higher. Although you can install professional burners purchased from a manufacturer in this kiln, the simple and inexpensive system described here has been in use for a number of years and has proved successful. Each burner is made up of commonly available pipe fittings which are put together like professional manufactured burners. A small amount of mechanical work is involved in placing a primary-air control disk across the front opening of the burners, but this simply entails tapping a ¼″ hole on the side of the opening to mount the disk. Do the mounting with a brass ¼″ round-headed screw, ½″ long, which holds the disk in place over the face of the 2″ galvanized tee opening.

A 24″ length of 2″ pipe, with a cap on one end and a 2″ gas control valve on the other, is the manifold on which the three burners are mounted. Place the manifold up against the burner ports on the outside of the kiln and make a mark on the manifold pipe to indicate the center of each burner port. These three marks must be in absolute alignment before you center-punch and drill them open to receive the individual ⅛″ gas pet cock for each of the three burners. Each location is drilled slightly undersize of a ⅛″ pipe fitting, and threaded. After the burners have been assembled, you can mount them onto the manifold, and then the manifold is mounted along the side of the kiln with the head of each burner projecting about 1″ into the burner port chamber. (Fig. 3–28.) Plumbers mounting straps can be used to hang the entire assembly onto the concrete cinder block foundation directly under the burner ports to ensure the burners being centered into the ports.

3–27.
Burner System

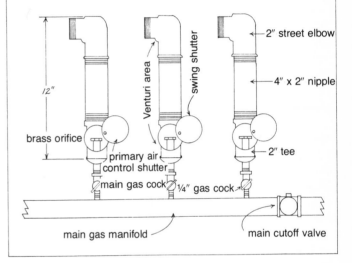

3 burners with primary air control shutter and individual gas-cock valve/brass-orifice plug. Each at 200,000 B.t.u./600,000 B.t.u. required.

2″ street elbow

4″ x 2″ nipple

12″

Venturi area

swing shutter

brass orifice

2″ tee

primary air control shutter

main gas cock ¼″ gas cock

main gas manifold

main cutoff valve

3–26. Floor bricks inside the kiln have perforated holes that allow heat to pass downward to the flue opening.

3–28. Each burner projects about one inch into the burner port chamber.

B.T.U.

The B.t.u. for operating this kiln to cone 10 and above is deliberately calculated to provide an "overpower" of heat input. In this sense, this kiln may be thought of as a vehicle with a souped-up engine. The reason for this is simply to provide absolute control of heat input and yet to have the flexibility of using any one or a combination of two burners to regulate the heat input. Using a rather standard measurement rule-of-thumb, 30,000 B.t.u. per cubic foot of kiln space is calculated to a total of 600,000 B.t.u. Divide this into three burners, thus giving each burner a maximum output of 200,000 B.t.u. for the 20 cubic feet of kiln space heated to cone 10. If you use liquid petroleum gas, you will need a No. 19($5/32''$ drill bit) orifice drill at 11 lbs.; if your fuel is a natural gas, use a $7/32''$ drill to get the right orifice size.

Flame and Firing

Since each burner has its own control gas valve, you have several alternatives available to you when you fire this kiln. For a pre-drying warm-up period, you can turn on only the center burner to a low-moderate position, thus preventing an excessive amount of heat from entering the kiln too suddenly. After the drying cycle is completed and temperatures have been brought up into the range—500° to 900°F.—which will eliminate chemical water in the pottery, you can increase the input of the center burner while keeping the other two burners in the same setting, in this way allowing the heat in the kiln to rise slowly until it reaches peak temperature. On the other hand, you could increase the flame input of all three burners to create a faster heat rise within the kiln and to trim the firing time of the entire cycle. During the heat input operation, the flame emitted from the burner should be a long, yellow, tiger-tailed flame with a small blue crown near the front of the burner nozzle. (See ch. 1 for a description of flame characteristics.) The primary-air control disk on the face of each burner sets the character and combustion of the flame. Normally, the most efficient setting of the primary-air control disk is about ½" open at sea level.

The typical firing chart in Figure 3–29 gives some notes and procedures for firing this kiln with natural gas, based upon years of experience in the control of this kiln at cone 10 and above under medium to heavy reduction conditions.

FIRING CHART

OPERATOR: _Colson_   KILN & FIRE NO. _R.A. #9_ DATE: _8/30/74_

TYPE FIRE: _A10 Reduction_   METER ON _652_ METER OFF _669_

TIME	GAS	NOTES: FLAME, DAMPER, ETC.	COLOR	TEMP.	MATH
7:15 am	—	2 outside burners on soft low (primaries off) open above top peep. Damp 3/4 open	Blk	—	
8:00 am	—	Door closed			
8:30 am	1/2	3 peeps closed, center burner on soft	Blk		
9:30 am	1	outside burner on soft (all primaries on)	Blk		
10:30 am	2	center burner up slightly	Blk		
11:30 am	3	outside burners up medium			
12:30 pm	5	first two burners up med-fast	Dull red	900°+	
1:30 pm	8	center burner on full and damper pushed in 1"	Cherry	1400°+	
2:30 pm	10	Reduction starting, damper in 3/4" more	orange	1850°+	
3:30 pm	14	*A5 starting, top and bottom	lemon	2100°+	
4:30 pm	16	*A5 down, A9 starting reduction continuing	yellow	2250°+	
5:00	17	*A9 flatout, A10 down to 3 o'clock. OFF	light yellow	2380°+	

3–29. A typical firing chart for firing the twenty-cubic-foot downdraft Roman arch kiln.

Materials List for the Twenty-Cubic-Foot Downdraft Roman Arch Kiln

Kiln base:
16 concrete cinder blocks (each 8″ x 8″ x 16″) (Blocks may be cemented together or left free.)

Brick:
All standard size straights (each 9″ x 4½″ x 2½″)
Floor:
100 hard refractory bricks, 2600°F. 15 sq. ft. compressed ceramic-fiber board, ½″ or ¼″ thick, 2600°F.
Walls and arch:
380 soft insulating bricks, 2600°F.
Interior floor:
20 hard refractory bricks—uprights for supporting open floor bricks, 2600°F.
Floor face:
20 bricks with holes, 2600°F.
Bag wall:
10 hard refractory bricks—baffle wall for firebox, 2600°F.
Flue:
25 hard refractory bricks—supporting bricks for flue liners, 2600°F.

Mortar:
100 lbs. fireclay—for making up slip for dipping bricks and for leveling

Arch support:
2 channel iron buttresses (each 33″ x 4″ x $^3/_{16}$″)
4 tie rods (45″ x ½″ diam.) round iron with ½″ nuts and ½″ washers

Kiln arch forms:
2 scrap wood boards used as main arch forms (each 38″ x 5″ x ¾″)
2 scrap wood boards used as horizontal supports (each 38″ x 4″ x ¾″)
18 wood slats (each 1½″ x ⅜″ or ¾″ x 23″)
4 scrap wood boards used for vertical upright supports (any size, such as 2″ x 2″, or 2″ x 4″, approximately 48″ long)
1 scrap wood board used for the door arch form only (25″ x 4″ x ¾″)

Thermal ceramic-fiber blanket:
75 sq. ft. alumina-silica, ½″ thick, 6 lb. density, 2300°F.

Flue liners:
4 (each 12″ x 12″ outside diam. 24″ high)
20′ plumbers metal strapping with holes
4 bolts with nuts for bolting straps (each ¼″ x 3″)
4 angle irons as support for flue liner (each 1½″ x ⅛″ x 8″)

Weather cover:
1 bag white cement (100 lbs.)
1 bag finishing sand (100 lbs.)
3 pieces lath wire, galvanized (each 2′ x 8′)
1 lb. roofing nails, wide flat head
1 roll bailing wire, approx. 20′

Burner parts (see Fig. 3–27):
3 street elbows, each 2″
3 nipples (each 2″ x 4″)
3 tees, each 2″
3 galvanized or brass disks, each 2″ diam.
3 round-head brass bolts (each ¼″ x ½″)
3 thick disk plates with ¾″ hole in center used to seal bottom of 2″ tee where gas mixer seats (each 2″ diam. by $^3/_{16}$)
3 galvanized nipples with thread on one end (each ½″ x 3″)
3 brass orifice caps, each ½″ (acquire from gas supplier)
3 gas cocks, each ⅛″
1 galvanized pipe with threads on both ends, 2″ x 24″ (this is the main manifold for mounting burners)
1 cap for end of burner manifold, 2″·
1 main gas valve for placing on incoming line, 2″

Damper shelf:
1 silicon-carbide or mullite shelf (16″ x 10½″ x 1″)

Ware shelves:
12 silicon-carbide shelves—(each 16″ x 13″ x ⅝″)

14 shelf supports:
Made by cutting hard refractory bricks in half down the center, lengthwise (each 9″ x 4½″ x 2½″). Cut pieces are again cut in halves, quarters, and three-quarters to make up assortment of posts. Use twenty 9″ straights for cutting these posts.

4. The Suspension Drum Kiln

This kiln, which is designed for cone 10 reduction, represents a radical departure from traditional kilns in that it provides the best combination of a suspension kiln along with superior thermal qualities. The kiln does not contain any bricks whatsoever, relying entirely upon ceramic-fiber materials recently developed for usage at higher temperatures.

The concept of a suspension device for heat containment, which can be raised or lowered to fit over a bed of materials, is not new; it has been used in metal tempering for years. In fact, a suspension device using standard refractory brick has even been adapted for firing and processing raku pottery. Dependence on dense, bulky, and heavy refractory insulating materials, however, has always required heavy mechanical operating devices. This drum kiln entirely eliminates the awkwardness of working with a heavy device, and it also offers a superior means of firing a moderate chamber area at low cost. The accessibility provided to the stack area is similar to that obtained in using a rolling car bed kiln.

The simplicity and effectiveness of this kiln are based upon two factors: it is an updraft kiln, and, being made entirely of the new materials, it is extremely light in weight. If you have gathered together all materials before starting construction, you can complete this kiln in one day.

The kiln utilizes a standard 55-gallon steel drum which is easily available and which provides a simple rigid casing to hold the pliable ceramic-fiber blanket in position during use. Although Figure 4–1 is based upon a 55-gallon steel drum, you can construct a proportionally larger kiln of this type in the same manner by using a larger steel casing. The 55-gallon steel drum, however, provides almost 7 cubic feet of easily accessible stacking space. The burner system is made of pipe fittings that accommodate either natural or liquid gas. Since the metal stand on which the base of this kiln rests is lightweight, it can easily be moved by hand for proper adjustment of the burner positions. The body of the kiln has a top so there is no lid.

Drum Shell Construction

The 55-gallon steel drum must be complete with both ends intact—not just on one end and sealed on the other. If you use an old drum, be sure to check for residue inside. Sometimes a drum has previously contained highly volatile material, such as lacquer thinner, polyester resin, or gasoline. Clean the drum thoroughly of such residue materials before cutting it with a torch. Normally, a large screw cap can be located on the lid of the drum; this can be removed to let out fumes of toxic residue and allow cleaning. You can use a garden hose, detergent, and water to clean out the inside of a drum, but if the residue is oily and difficult to remove, it may be necessary to use a grease-cutting cleaner. Plastic compound residues such as polyester resin are very difficult to remove, so it is best to acquire a drum that did not hold this type material.

Once the inside of the drum has been flushed out and is free of residue, cut it into two sections: one will make up the base and the other the kiln body suspension cover.

Scribe a line 5″ from one end of the drum to mark the division of the two sections. Make the marking with a sharp-pointed metal instrument that will scratch into the surface of the metal, particularly if cutting is to be done with a torch. However, if the cutting will be mechanical, a pencil line is sufficient for the purpose. Mechanical cutting can be accomplished by drilling several holes touching one another in a straight line. Next, insert an electric saber saw with a metal cutting blade; you can maintain excellent cutting control with this technique. If you cut by hand, a pointed metal-cutting saw is suggested; although quite tedious, this technique can accomplish the same result as the saber saw.

4–1.
Suspension Drum Kiln

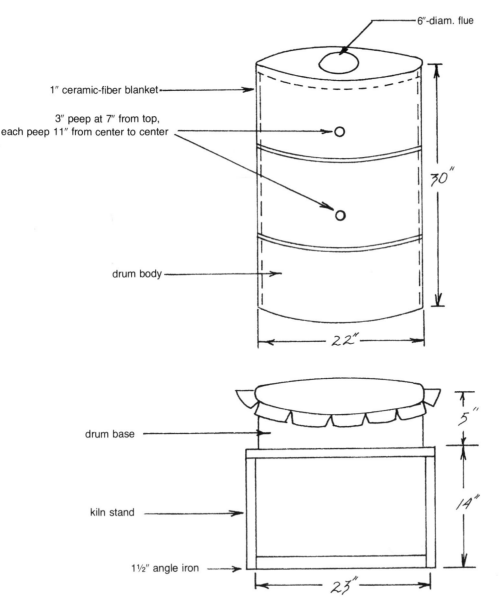

6″-diam. flue

1″ ceramic-fiber blanket

3″ peep at 7″ from top,
each peep 11″ from center to center

drum body

30″

22″

drum base

5″

kiln stand

14″

1½″ angle iron

23″

The Drum Base (Firebox)

The short section cut away from the drum functions as the kiln firebox and supporting floor for the bottom shelf of the stack area in the kiln. From the open-ended edge of this section, scribe a line 2″ below the cut. Every 5″ or 6″, cut a notch with a pair of metal shears to the scribed line. (Fig. 4–2.) After you have notched the entire circumference of this edge, bend each section between notches outward to a 90° angle. (Fig. 4–3.) When covered with ceramic-fiber material, this extended lip will provide a seating position for the drum body after the entire assembly has been put together.

All four burner ports must now be measured and cut. Each hole is 3″ in diameter and located on the bottom of the drum-base form. Scribe the proper position for the burner ports from Figure 4–4. Cut the holes out in the same manner that the drum was cut into two sections.

Roll out a section of ceramic-fiber blanket and place the drum base upon the blanket. Press the base into the blanket and then remove it. The imprint that the base leaves upon the blanket indicates the correct size of the base and the burner port openings. (Fig. 4–5.) Cut out the area indicated on the blanket with a pair of heavy-duty scissors to form a ceramic-fiber disk. (Fig. 4–6.) The disk should be cut out approximately ¼″ inside the line of the marked area, in order to compensate for the extended area of the metal rim when the initial measurement was taken and to allow for a proper fit inside the base frame. Figure 4–6 shows a ceramic-fiber blanket containing a metal-foil backing; this material is laid into the bottom of the drum base, metal foil downward, so as to help protect the underside of the blanket at the burner-port openings during firing operations. Although desirable, a metal-foil backed blanket is not absolutely necessary; a standard blanket, with a rigidizing surface, will serve the same purpose. (Rigidizing is discussed in ch. 8.)

Now cut a piece of ½″ ceramic-fiber compressed board and place it on top of the blanket material which has already been seated into the drum base. Mark the ceramic-fiber board the same way you did the blanket. However, you should shape the board with a sharp cutting blade, such as a Stanley cutting-edge knife. (Fig. 4–7.) Ceramic-fiber board is normally only available in one-foot-wide sections; therefore it will be necessary to piece the board in order to make it fit properly into the drum base. Both the board and the blanket at this point are materials rated at 2300°F. usage—that is, their "hot face"

4–2. The drum kiln base has notches cut every 5 or 6″ with metal shears.

4–3. Each notched tongue is bent outward to a 90° angle.

usage temperature, not their melting temperature, is 2300°F. (Fig. 4–8.)

After these two layers of insulating material have been inserted, put in a third layer of material used to complete construction of the drum base: a 1″ ceramic-fiber blanket rated at 2600°F. for high-temperature usage. This final piece, which will take the brunt of excessive heat generated in the firebox area, should be larger in diameter than the pieces already inserted and should extend to the outside edge of the bent flange of the drum base. It must be thoroughly secured into the drum base with an application of sodium silicate or ceramic-fiber liquid cement. Paint the adhesive onto the metal face of the notched flange and press the blanket down firmly.

4–4.

Burner for Drum Kiln

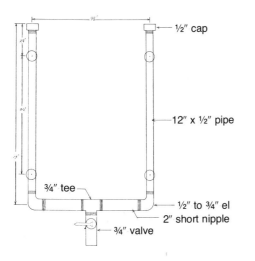

½″ cap

12″ x ½″ pipe

¾″ tee

½″ to ¾″ el

2″ short nipple

¾″ valve

4–5. A section of ceramic-fiber blanket is rolled out to allow the drum base to leave an imprint of its circumference.

4–6. The area indicated on the blanket by the drum base may be cut out with scissors.

4–7. Ceramic-fiber board may be cut with a sharp blade to the shape of the drum base.

4–8. A ceramic-fiber board is placed above a layer of ceramic-fiber blanket.

The total thickness of the three insulating materials will be 2″. This "beefing up" of insulation in the drum base serves the purpose of reflecting a greater amount of heat up from the firebox into the kiln and results in better firing efficiency. It also protects the bottom metal retaining form from warping and becoming weak due to excessive heat exposure.

Once the drum base is complete, the burner ports can be cut out. Using a long-bladed sharp knife, puncture the blanket from underneath the base while at the same time supporting the inside lining with one hand to prevent any possible pushing out of the inserted material. Following the contour of the metal hole, use the blade in a sawing motion to cut out a plug. This opening is the burner port. After all four ports have been cut out, press the rough exposed edge of ceramic fiber in with the fingers to create a smooth edge. The edge can then be painted with a ceramic-fiber liquid cement to strengthen and protect it from usage.

The Drum Body

The remaining portion of the steel drum measures 30″ long. Before beginning the job of lining the drum with ceramic-fiber blanket, the inside walls and lid area must be thoroughly cleaned of any residue to assure the best possible adhesion of the insulating material to the inside metal surface.

At this time the flue and two peepholes should be cut out. The flue is a circular hole in the top of the drum measuring 6″ in diameter, and there is one 3″ peephole for each section of the drum body—upper and lower. (See Fig. 4–1.)

The completed drum body is lined with a layer of 1″-thick high-temperature ceramic-fiber blanket rated at 2600°F. The inside ceiling disk, which is the first piece placed inside the drum body, must be measured and fitted very carefully. If it is not secured well, after several firings it will separate from its metal facing and fall down into the ware or top baffle plate. Placing this disk in the ceiling of the drum body first will help the wall insulation hold its outer edges in position.

Measure the diameter of this ceiling insulation by placing the drum body, top down, upon a piece of rolled out ceramic-fiber blanket. Press the drum down slightly, so that when you remove it, it leaves an impression in the blanket which will clearly indicate the cutting line. Cut the disk out with a pair of scissors ¼″ short of the cutting line

to allow for the difference between the outside and inside edge of the metal drum. Next, with the open end of the drum up, paint a heavy coating of sodium silicate liquid or ceramic-fiber liquid cement onto the inside of the drum lid. Gently place the blanket disk down on the wet surface and press firmly against the inner metal surface with the palms of the hands to help adhere the material to the metal surface. This piece of material will remain in place while you move the drum body about for the installation of the wall blanket. Do *not* cut the flue hole out of the blanket before installation.

To determine the correct length of the blanket needed to line the inside of the drum wall, measure the outside circumference and deduct about 3″ to compensate for the inside measurement. This figure will total approximately 6′. The depth of the drum body is 30″, but the blanket should be at least 3″ longer, to lap over the edge outside the drum body. Since standard high-temperature blankets are normally furnished in rolls of one- or two-foot widths, you will have to piece the blanket together carefully inside the drum wall so as not to allow heat to escape through the adjoining seams.

Measure the circumference on a section of ceramic-fiber blanket that has been rolled out flat and cut. (Fig. 4–9.) Roll up the cut blanket gently so that it can easily fit inside the drum. Insert and unroll it completely against the inner wall. This procedure constitutes an important dry run to check that the measurement has been made properly. The two ends of the blanket roll should meet with a very snug seam. If there is a small overlap, push the material back and compress it to make the ends conform tightly. If the blanket turns out short and leaves a small gap, you can cut and insert a narrow strip of blanket into the gap after the blanket is permanently installed.

Now reroll the blanket inside the drum and gently remove it. Paint the inside of the drum body liberally with ceramic-fiber coating cement or liquid sodium silicate. Replace the rolled-up blanket in the drum, carefully unrolling it up against the inside of the coated wall. (Fig. 4–10.) After the blanket has been completely unrolled, press the entire surface gently with the palms of the hands. If another roll, cut to the proper width, is needed, place it tightly up against the initial roll and proceed with installation in the same manner. When the lining is completed, the blanket should extend out of the bottom end of the drum approximately 3″. Now notch this extension with a pair of scissors about every 4 to 5″ and curl each piece over the drum edge, pressing it against the outside metal surface. (Fig. 4–11.)

Beginning just under the extended area of the blanket, also paint the drum's outside surface with high-temperature adhesive glue and press the material upon it for stability. You can anchor this exterior layer of ceramic-fiber blanket further with a metal strap or wire which you bind tightly around the drum's circumference. (Fig. 4–12.) Since this area does not receive direct heat exposure, the metal binding strap will not be affected.

After the inside of the drum body has been lined, the drum can be turned right side up for completion. To assure that the ceiling material inside the drum will not work loose during subsequent firings, insert pieces of high-temperature Nichrome or stainless steel wire through the top to anchor the blanket. On top of the drum, around the flue hole, drill a series of small ⅛″-holes every two inches. Thread a substantial length of Nichrome wire through one of the holes and back through the lining underneath, up through the next hole, and so on. This mechanical-wire sewing will assure a solid anchoring of the ceiling blanket along the edge of the flue opening.

4–10. The ceramic-fiber blanket is rolled out gently against the inside of the coated drum body.

4–11. The notched ceramic-fiber blanket extensions are curled over the edge against the outside of the drum body.

4–12. The blanket exterior can be anchored in place with a metal strap.

4–9. A roll of ceramic-fiber blanket is measured at six feet for the drum lining.

The peep and flue holes can be cut out in the same way as the burner ports. (Fig. 4–13.)

To complete the top of the drum body installation, cut a disk of foil-backed blanket to conform to the outside top of the drum body. The top has a small lip that extends ½" above the lid inside which the blanket will fit snugly. Cut a plug out of this material to form the flue hole opening. The drum lid is now sandwiched between a 1"-thick piece of high-temperature blanket on the inside and a ½"-thick piece of 2300°F.-temperature blanket on the outside. This triple insulated top enhances heat reflection during firing cycles when temperatures are high and protects the metal lid from warping. The blanket you use here does not have to have metal-foil backing; a normal ½" ceramic-fiber thermal blanket can be used with a top application of rigidizing liquid and a coat of ceramic-fiber liquid cement as a waterproof weather protector. It is important to insulate the top of the drum as just described since a great deal of thermal abuse occurs at this location during firings to high temperatures.

4–13. The peepholes are cut out with a sharp blade.

Peephole Covers

Instead of plugs which are normally used with brick kilns, the peepholes on this kiln have hinged covers. A small metal hinge is brazed or mechanically screwed into a 4" x 6" piece of galvanized sheet metal. Glue a square of ceramic-fiber blanket onto the underside of the metal plate, and then mount this upon the face of the drum body just above the peephole opening. The mounting is done by attaching the opposite end of the hinge to the drum face with sheet metal screws or by brazing. (Fig. 4–14.)

Directly under the plate, loop a ⅛"-piece of steel welding rod on one end and mount it with a washer and sheet metal screw. (See Fig. 4–14.) Keep the mounting screw loose so the rod can be moved sideways to unlock the peep flap and lifted to inspect the inside of the kiln. Leave the blanket soft, not rigidized, so that it will seat itself snugly against the peep opening when it is closed. (Fig. 4–15.) An alternative to the rigid rod is a piece of spring steel rod that can be sprung back to the peep cover. In closing, the rod is simply "snapped" back onto the cover.

Rigidizing and Sealing

Except for the compressed ceramic-fiber board sandwiched into the drum base, the rest of the kiln is lined entirely with ceramic-fiber blanket which can easily be damaged because of its fragile fibrous makeup. However, the blanket's thermal capabilities compensate well for this lack of tensile strength. Moreover, the surface of the material can be considerably improved with application of liquid ridigizer. Ceramic-fiber rigidizer, a nonorganic binder with a consistency much like that of water, increases hardness of the material to which it is applied and improves resistance to erosion. All interior surfaces of the drum kiln should be coated with a rigidizer liquid, and spraying is the easiest way of doing it. However, if spray equipment is not available, you can apply rigidizer by brushing or sponging. (Fig. 4–16.) With this type of application you will need a great deal more rigidizer liquid since the blanket surface acts much like a sponge, but the heavy application will not be harmful to the blanket since the liquid saturates deeper into the material than in spray application. Since the blanket absorbs liquid so readily, it will take a considerable amount of time for the rigidizer to dry and stiffen the surface. After applying the rigidizer, you can smooth the blanket surface with a roller. (Fig. 4–17.)

Should you put the kiln into operation before the

rigidizer is dry, a low flame will accelerate the drying process and not harm the blanket.

Any areas, seams, joints, or unmatched insulated sections within the kiln can be patched at this time. Wet ceramic-fiber material can easily be molded to shapes and contours or, where needed, flattened and flanged for sealing purposes. You can simply cut a scrap piece of blanket, saturate it with rigidizer, and press it into position for sealing. For example, you can press a strip of blanket along the circular joint where the inside wall blanket butts against the ceiling blanket covering to form a beveled heat seal. The same can be done along any other seams within the kiln where joints meet.

After the rigidizer has completely dried, leaving a stiff rigid surface, you can paint ceramic-fiber liquid cement on top of the rigid surface to further increase both the blanket's strength and its insulating qualities. However, the liquid cement is quite different from the rigidizer in that it has a heavy, thick consistency, almost like that of yogurt. (For more on this material, see ch. 8.)

4–14. The peephole is covered with a piece of sheet metal and a hinge, which is then covered with ceramic-fiber blanket.

4–15. The underside of the hinged peep cover is left pliable.

4–16. Rigidizer liquid is being applied to the ceramic-fiber surface with a sponge.

4–17. After the rigidizer is applied, the surface of the blanket is smoothed with a roller.

Kiln Stand

As depicted in Figure 4–1, the drum base rests upon an angle-iron stand. This stand is a frame made of 1″ angle iron welded together to create an open box measuring 14″ high by 23″ square. The 23″-square measurement should fit the outside circumference of the kiln drum, with the kiln base seating comfortably inside the lip of the angle iron. This fit assures that the drum base will not shift in any way after it has been aligned with the drum body and burner system. The stand provides the necessary space under the drum base for the burner system.

Burners

Four small burners made up of pipe fittings furnish the heat input for this kiln. (See Fig. 4–4.) If the kiln is operated with liquid propane gas, use a size 48 orifice drill. Each burner will produce 45,450 B.t.u. input at full capacity, resulting in a total of 181,800 B.t.u. A ⅛″ drill bit will provide an orifice opening with an input of 50,000 B.t.u. for each burner using natural gas, supplying a total of 200,000 B.t.u. for this kiln.

The burner system is designed to utilize the least parts for the most effect. Figure 4–4 illustrates a U-shaped manifold, which contains a gas-valve pet cock on one end and allows each burner to be mounted upright on its extending arms. The orifice holes for each burner must be drilled and in the right place on the manifold before you mount the burners. To assure correct alignment with the burner ports in the drum base, place the burner manifold flush under the drum base and mark the centers of the burners on the manifold through the burner ports from within the drum base.

The entire burner system operates on an atmospheric natural draft principle in the same way as described in chapter 2 for the twelve-cubic-foot catenary kiln. The use of oil or other heavy-fuel system would require larger burner ports and a burner system utilizing a heavy fuel for proper operation of this kiln.

Mount the burner system under the drum kiln in one of three ways: Strap it onto the kiln stand with plumbers mounting straps; if the entire system is steady and the burners are in proper alignment to the burner ports, prop it up with bricks or blocks under the manifold (Fig. 4–18); or suspend it by means of connecting the main incoming gas line to the main control valve.

The burner heads should be centered in relation to the burner ports and not more than ¼″ below the opening of each port. (Review burner characteristics in ch. 1.)

Drum Suspension System

In order to arrange the mounting equipment for suspending the drum kiln, you will need an area at least eight feet high and only 2½ feet wide. If there is no natural device for hanging a pulley-cable system, such as a tree or roof overhang, an overhead structure must be constructed of wood beams.

Two 10′ x 4″ x 4″ treated posts, counter sunk two feet into the ground, serve the purpose of stabilizing the upright timber. Pour a mixture of concrete around the base of the posts to assure stability. A crossbeam must be secured across the top of the vertical beams. To further support and stabilize the entire structure, eye hooks can be anchored and guide wires brought down and pegged into the earth or floor surface.

Place two pulleys on the structure, both with metal—not nylon—center wheels, so that they will be unaffected by heat coming from the top of the kiln during operation. Bolt one pulley directly to the center of the crossbeam; secure the other to the crossbeam's outside end.

For suspending the kiln, use a ³⁄₁₆″- or ¼″-thick stainless steel cable; this cable will have sufficient tensile strength not to be affected by heat of several hundred degrees. Since the cable does not remain over the top of the kiln during operation, it is not crucial that it be heat resistant.

The cable should measure at least 12′ long to run through the two pulleys from a ratchet winch located on the side to the top of the drum. A small, simple lightweight boat winch will serve well for drawing the drum up and letting it down into position. To assure stabilization of the drum while in suspension, you should be able to lock and unlock this winch during operation. It is helpful to have the winch located near enough so that you can hand-guide the kiln into position when lowering it onto its base.

If you wish, the cable can have a counterweight instead of a winch. It should be approximately equal in weight to the drum body, so that when the weight is pulled down, the drum body will rise and stay in any given position, and when it is lifted, the drum body will lower itself smoothly and evenly on the drum base. The counterweight can be a bundle of bricks, a piece of heavy iron, or a sandbag.

The remaining cable is threaded through the pulley located on the outside of the vertical supporting beam and then through the center crossbeam pulley directly over the drum. Then draw the cable through the eye of a snap hook and bolt it securely with two small U-bolts. Now the cable is ready to be attached to the drum-suspension assembly, which consists of three 12″ turnbuckles.

Bore three ⅜″-holes through the extending lip, which is almost ¾″ above the top of the kiln drum body, at equal distances to one another and slightly oversize. Into each of these holes, place a 12″ x ⅜″-diameter turnbuckle. The turnbuckles must have an open hook on one end and a closed loop at the other. (Fig. 4–19.) When you place the turnbuckle into the drum hole, the hook must face outward because if it is in the reverse position, it will not ride downward to the center of the kiln to connect with the snap hook. The snap hook, which is attached to the cable from the pulleys, is pulled down into position for connecting with the three turnbuckles. (Fig. 4–20.) When the drum is lifted up, the turnbuckles can be hand adjusted for leveling—that is, screwed in or out. When the drum is down and seated on the base, detach the snap hook and pull the turnbuckles out away from the flue opening. (Fig. 4–21.) You can also easily remove them from the kiln if necessary.

Take care not to damage the ceramic-fiber surface overlapped at the bottom of the drum body as you attach the cable and turnbuckle. During lifting, the drum will tend to rotate slightly, but this is no major problem since you can turn it by hand until it matches its seating position on the drum base.

4–18. The burner system is held in position with bricks under the manifold.

4–19. In the mounting position, the hook ends of the turnbuckles must face outward. (Turnbuckle innovation by Charles Maggio.)

4–20. The snap hook is drawn down from above and the turnbuckles placed into it.

4–21. The turnbuckles may be turned out during firings to avoid heat from the flue.

Drum Body and Base Alignment

After the kiln drum body is attached to the pulley turnbuckle cable system, lift and lower it several times to check for level and even movement. If all is satisfactory, then the kiln stand, along with the drum base, can be placed under the suspended drum body. Lower the drum body to an inch or two above the top of the drum base; there alignment is made to assure that the drum body seats itself snugly on the flange of the kiln drum base. At this point, it is important to be certain that the fit is absolute; this area is the firebox and there should be no opportunity for heat to escape along the perimeter of this seam.

There are two ways to assure proper seating of the kiln drum body with the drum base flange. One way is to place the drum body on top of the drum base ceramic-fiber surface *before* you apply a rigidizer. The weight of the body will make an indenture on top of the ceramic-fiber base flange and create a natural concave contour. Once this contour is well defined, you can rigidize the ceramic-fiber material at this location.

A second way to seal the bottom of the drum is to attach three metal tongues to the bottom of the drum body with matching tongues on the drum base. When you lower the drum body into position, clamp the matching tongues together with a small C clamp.

Firing Procedure

To understand the operating characteristics of the suspension drum kiln, it is necessary to recognize that it is an updraft system. You must also be aware that if care is not taken, the ceramic-fiber insulation, although substantially strengthened with rigidizer, is vulnerable to damage during operation, particularly during loading and unloading. (See the description of ceramic-fiber characteristics in the Introduction.)

First, arrange the kiln's firebox area by placing three 4″ hard refractory brick posts into the bottom drum base at equal distances to one another. (Fig. 4–22.) Being spongy, the face of the ceramic-fiber floor will give at first, but the material will "settle in" and remain stable once it has absorbed the pressure from the weight of the shelves that have been installed above. Place the fire-wall shelf upon the posts. This shelf—15½″ square, either of silicon-carbide or mullite—acts as the primary reflecting baffle against the flames from the burners underneath. Be careful that the shelf corners do not puncture or scrape the inner wall lining of the drum body when you lower it down

into a locking position with the drum base. You may have to cut corners off of the shelves to prevent this type of damage, and this should be done before you first begin to operate the kiln. On top of the fire-wall baffle shelf, place three small refractory shims, not more than ½″ thick, directly over the posts below. Place a second shelf identical to the first on top of the shims. (See Fig. 4–23.) This second shelf becomes the bottom ware stacking area of the kiln.

Since updraft kilns normally have hot bottoms because of the placement of the firebox, it is important to protect ware on the bottom shelf from excessive heat with the double baffle described. To allow optimum heat circulation, all shelves above the firebox baffle shelf should be "split" except the very top shelf. Each split shelf is half the size of the firebox baffle shelf, and there are two split shelves on each level. (Fig. 4–23.) A modification of this arrangement is to stagger the split shelves so that no two shelves meet at the same level. If half round shelves are available, heat flow and circulation will be easier to handle, but rectangular shelves will suffice as long as their corners do not damage or obstruct the inner ceramic-fiber wall. Figure 4–23 illustrates how the divided shelves are placed so as to allow heat and flame circulation to be driven up through the center of the kiln. Therefore, the flame emerges initially through the burner ports, strikes the lower fire-wall baffle shelf, follows a path along the outside of this shelf, up the wall of the drum and into the center of the kiln. From there it goes up through the center openings of the split shelves and underneath the top flue baffle shelf, where it finally appears along the outer edges of this shelf and emerges out of the flue opening at the top of the kiln. This shelf arrangement accomplishes three things: It protects the ware in the bottom of the kiln from getting overheated; it directs heat circulation into the center of the kiln, thus inhibiting substantial heat loss along the inside walls; and it retards the escape of heat out the flue opening by holding the heat under the full baffle shelf just a few inches below the top of the kiln. This arrangement, developed with considerable effort and over a long period of time, best controls and utilizes the upward driving circulation of heat in a small confined kiln of this nature.

The new materials used for this kiln absorb almost no heat. Heat-absorbing refractory materials are important in helping to return radiant heat into the kiln space during the cooling cycle after temperature has been reached. Essentially, the only sources of returnable heat available in this kiln are the refractory shelves, posts, and the ware. Keep these factors in mind after you shut the kiln off if you do not down fire.

The total firing cycle period for reaching an even saturation of stoneware temperature should not be less than eight hours; allow the ware an opportunity to reach temperature slowly and evenly for good glaze flow and smooth finishes. However, with this kiln, it may prove difficult to keep the firing cycle going as long as eight hours. If the kiln is fired too rapidly, heat will be exceedingly uneven and there will be considerable differences in cone droppage, in spite of the recommended shelf arrangement. Therefore, a list of suggestions for firing the suspension drum kiln follows. As mentioned in previous chapters, you need at least eight to ten firings before you reach a point of understanding and control of any one particular kiln. Small discoveries during operation will substantially help you to fire an individual kiln with success.

4–22. After the last layer of blanket is secured in the drum base, three 4″ hard refractory posts are placed between the burner ports to support the bottom shelf.

4–23.
Suspension Drum Kiln Stacking Arrangement and Heat Circulation

6″ flue

15½″ full round shelf

post

1″ ceramic-fiber blanket insulation (2600°F.)

double baffle shelf

½″ refractory shim

firebox

Operation Checklist

1. During low-fire pre-heat cycle, try to avoid too much smoke appearing out of the flue opening; it may be necessary to allow a small amount of smoke, but not more than that.

2. A damper, cut from a piece of compressed ceramic-fiber board, can be used to close down the flue as much as halfway during the early pre-heat cycles. This damper must be opened as heat increases within the kiln, although no valve adjustment may have to be made. A slab of hard refractory shelving will also serve well as a damper.

3. You can increase fuel input little by little without causing flame to appear out of the flue, but only to the point of maximum efficiency. (See the definition of maximum fuel efficiency in ch. 1.)

4. During the high-fire cycle, when the gas input valve is in its highest position, do not allow a large quantity of flame to appear out of the flue opening. Six inches would be maximum.

5. Allow heat to build up in phases of at least one hour. Unless absolutely necessary, do not make valve or damper adjustments in between these times.

6. Let heat saturate as long as possible—1½ to 4 hours—before giving the last boost of fuel to reach final temperature.

7. After reaching temperature and shutting off the kiln, close all openings to the kiln to help contain heat during the cooling cycle.

8. Too rapid cooling following completion of firing can result in glazes looking unsettled (rough or bubbly), and cause undue stress on kiln shelves as well as pots.

9. For "down firing," the following procedures is recommended: After reaching temperature, reduce the heat input until there is no back pressure and no flame coming out of the flue. Keep the flue wide open at this time, and hold this position for a minimum of one hour. After this hour, reset the valve so that the heat input is the same as at the pre-heat level. Hold this position for thirty minutes with the flue closed. At the end of this period, shut the kiln off completely and close up all openings.

10. If you are using LPG, keep the fuel tank as close as possible to maximum capacity (80 percent or better). Tank freezing can occur both as a result of high altitude as well as cold air temperature. Do not ever fire when the tank is below 30 percent capacity.

11. A clear, clean atmosphere inside the kiln indicates an oxidizing firing. A complete lack of smoke in the kiln is best for early heat-up stages.

12. A foggy atmosphere inside the kiln indicates that reduction is taking place.

13. Back pressure due to increased heat results in excessive flame shooting out of the flue. This may be released by leaving open a peephole which acts as a secondary flue.

14. A cone impregnated with heavy smoke will give an incorrect heat reading and also cause the cone to bend in an unconventional manner.

15. You can avoid flame licks upon ware by either using baffles or, if you use tiles, by stacking them so they face the center of the kiln.

16. Flame coming out of flue should be kept trimmed to within 3″ at the high end of the firing cycle. Do not allow greater flame output, since this indicates forcing fuel through the kiln and not containing the heat within it.

17. Always keep notes on firing cycles; these can be used as references to avoid mistakes and predict firings in advance.

Materials List for the Suspension Drum Kiln (Cone 10 Reduction)

Kiln shell:
One 55-gallon steel drum with both ends intact

Thermal blanket for drum body and drum base:
26 sq. ft. high-temperature (2600°F.) ceramic-fiber blanket, 1″ thick, 8 lb. density
12 sq. ft. standard ceramic-fiber blanket, ½″ thick, 6 lb. density, 2300°F. (foil-backed blanket is optional)
4 sq. ft. ceramic-fiber compressed board, ½″ thick, 2300°F.

Rigidizer:
½ gallon nonorganic liquid bonding (colloidal silica)
1 quart ceramic-fiber liquid cement, 2000°F.

Kiln stand:
8 pieces angle iron (each 1″ x ⅛″ x 23″)
4 pieces angle iron for uprights (each 1″ x ⅛″ x 14″)

Peephole covers:
2 pieces 4″ x 6″ flat sheet metal
Two 3″ metal hinges
2 self-tapping sheet metal screws
2 welding rods with loop on one end, ⅛″ diam.

Suspension hardware:
3 turnbuckles (each 12″ x ⅜″), open one end, closed loop opposite end
12 ft. stainless steel twisted cable, $3/16$ or ¼″ diam.
2 U-bolts for clasping cable (each 1″ x ¼″)
1 snap hook (4½″ metal)
1 ratchet boat winch or counterweight
2 pulleys, each 3″ with hanging loop, metal inner wheel
2 eye bolts (each ⅜″ diam. x 6″)
(Not shown in Fig. 4–1, these bolts are for securing the pulleys upon the crossbeam and vertical upright beams supporting the drum.)

Suspension beams:
2 treated beams for uprights (each 4″ x 4″ x 10′)
1 treated beam for crossbeam (4″ x 4″ x 38″)
(Optional: guy lines and accompanying hardware)

Burner parts:
two ½″ galvanized caps
2 galvanized pipes with thread at both ends (each ½″ x 12″)
2 galvanized elbows (each ¾″ x ½″)
2 galvanized nipples (each ¾″ x 3″)
One ¾″ galvanized tee
One ¾″ galvanized close nipple
4 galvanized nipples (burners, each 1½″ x 4″)
One ¾″ brass gas pet cock, female thread at both ends
1 tube of pipe thread caulking compound

Shelves and posts:
2 firebox baffle wall shelves, silicon-carbide, each 15½″ square with 3″ corners cut off. (These 2 shelves serve as bottom firebox shelves with a small spacer between them.)
3 stacking ware shelves, each 15½″ diam. full round by ⅝″ thick, cut into halves
50 posts, 1¼″ diam. round, varying in height from 1″ to 1½″
(These posts' convex and concave ends accommodate interlocking stacking to increase height of support.)

5. The Portable Raku Kiln

The portable raku kiln operates on the same principle as the drum kiln except that it is smaller and completely portable. (Fig. 5–1.) Two important factors contribute to the portability of this kiln: it is relatively small and it is extremely lightweight—a total of 10 pounds. These two characteristics provide a flexibility not usually available in kilns. It can be transported in an automobile and used on location. (Fig. 5–2.) It can also be operated in an area used for other activities, then stored away. The kiln's simple design and the components that operate it—the blower/burner and portable gas tank—provide an effective raku kiln at very little cost for materials and equipment.

The history of raku—a technique of doing instantaneous pottery—goes back to the age-old Japanese tea ceremony in which an unfired clay vessel is heat treated in an extremely simple and fast manner. Traditionally, an empty kiln is preheated to a glowing temperature of some 1,800 to 2,000°F. and the cold vessel, usually a tea bowl, is placed into the heated kiln. After a few minutes the glaze, which was previously placed on the vessel, melts and becomes buttery smooth. The vessel is removed from the kiln with a pair of metal tongs, and, still glowing with its molten glaze, is immediately buried in a container of organic matter, which may consist of dried leaves, straw, or wood shavings. The reaction of the hot vessel causes the matter to burn, affecting the coloration of the glaze. After a minute or two in the organic substance, the vessel is removed and plunged into a container of water. The water immediately "freezes" the glaze and the vessel is born.

5–2. The entire kiln, fuel tank, and burner system can be transported in a small auto.

5–1. The portable raku kiln.

Traditional kilns, even ancient ones, are consistently preheated to the necessary raku temperature of 1,800 to 2,000°F. This temperature is held in the kiln throughout the duration of the raku process, even while several vessels are treated.

The new raku kiln discussed in this chapter has such a radically different makeup from traditional kilns that an entirely different approach must be used in operating the kiln for raku pottery. Ceramic-fiber insulation materials retain very little of the incoming heat in the kiln chamber; more than 90 percent of the heat input driven into a ceramic-fiber lined container is contained without heat absorption. This eliminates the necessity to build heat up. If, in addition, the heat is forced into the chamber quite rapidly, there is minimal loss through the wall of the ceramic fiber. Therefore, instead of placing a raku vessel into a preheated kiln, as was previously done, the vessel is placed into an unlit raku kiln, the kiln turned on, and a temperature of 1,800°F. or better is reached in less than five seconds. It would take a conventional kiln hours to reach the same temperature level. The effect upon the raku ware is exactly the same as if it had been suddenly placed into a preheated kiln. Since raku temperatures are reached so quickly, it becomes totally unnecessary to leave the kiln turned on when you remove a raku vessel from the chamber. By cutting off the kiln before removing the raku vessel, the kiln operator is not exposed to a blast of heat when he opens the kiln. The only major source of heat being radiated comes from the raku vessel itself, not the kiln.

Operating this raku kiln results in the same effect on the pottery as has traditionally been sought and, moreover, does not require excessive fuel consumption, long heat-up periods, and is not awkward to handle.

Form Construction and Lining

The portable raku kiln is made up of three components: the heat chamber, the forced-air burner system, and the fuel tank. In constructing this kiln, the first consideration is the heat chamber. A ten-gallon galvanized garbage can constitutes the shell for the chamber. Use a new can to avoid residue and other foreign matter found in a used can and to assure good adhesion of the ceramic-fiber blanket to the inside of the can. The can lid must have a flue opening on top 5″ in diameter. Remove the handle at the top of the lid, if it has one, and cut the flue with a pair of metal cutting shears. (Fig. 5–3.) First, drill a series of ¼″

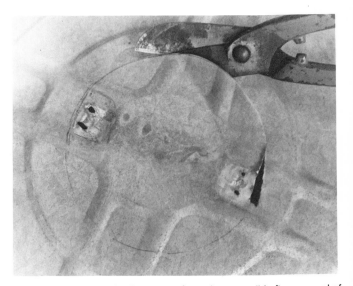

5–3. The 5″ flue opening is cut out of a garbage can lid after removal of the top handle.

holes into the lid along the perimeter line indicating the circular flue cut. If broken through into each other, these holes, provide an opening where the shear blade can begin its cut.

The burner hole is located at the bottom of the can floor and is oval in shape. A piece of 2″ galvanized or black iron pipe 14″ long, can be used as a guide. Scribe the circumference on the side 1″ from the floor of the can. Cut the opening as a circle initially before elongating it into an oval with the shears to assure that the hole is large enough for the 2″ pipe to slip through it. (Fig. 5–4.) Elongate the hole an additional 2″. Place the pipe into the hole again until it fits comfortably at an angle, which will allow the flame from the burner to follow a circular path inside the kiln chamber, thus increasing heat efficiency. (Fig. 5–5.)

The entire kiln contains only two holes: one in the lid for the flue; the other at the bottom of the container for the insertion of the burner. Peepholes in the side of the container are not needed since you can see the raku ware in the kiln through the flue opening on top.

Lining of the container and the lid is accomplished in the following manner. Measure a disk of ceramic-fiber blanket by pressing the bottom of the garbage-can container onto the surface of rolled-out material. (Fig. 5–6.) Cut the material out with a pair of scissors, and place the disk into the bottom of the garbage can. No high-temperature adhesive is needed. Next, cut a length of blanket measuring 43″ by 18″ and roll this piece up gently, taking care not to abuse the blanket surface. Then insert the blanket into the container against the inner wall (Fig. 5–7); unroll the blanket and check that both ends meet with a slight overlap. Note that the blanket will extend 2″ higher than the lip of the can. Remove the blanket from the container in the same manner that you inserted it. The inside wall of the container should now be painted with a very liberal application of sodium-silicate solution or ceramic-fiber liquid cement. Be sure the entire inner surface of the container is coated before you place the blanket back inside. (Fig. 5–8.) Return the rolled-up blanket to the inside chamber, set it against the coated wall, and carefully unroll it, while at the same time gently pressing it with the palms of the hands to assure that it has complete contact with the high-temperature liquid glue. Snip the extended blanket into 5″ sections to create tabs around the top of the can. (Fig. 5–9.) Glue the tabs down over the top rim after bending them over the container's lip.

5–4. The burner hole is cut as an oblong to accommodate the 2″-diameter burner.

5–5. The burner is placed through the kiln wall in such a manner as to allow the flame to follow a circular path.

5–6. The kiln container is placed upon the ceramic fiber to indicate the size of material to be cut.

5–7. The ceramic-fiber blanket is unrolled against the container's inner wall.

5–8. The entire inner face of the container is coated with sodium silicate before placing the blanket inside.

5–9. The blanket extension is snipped into 5″ sections.

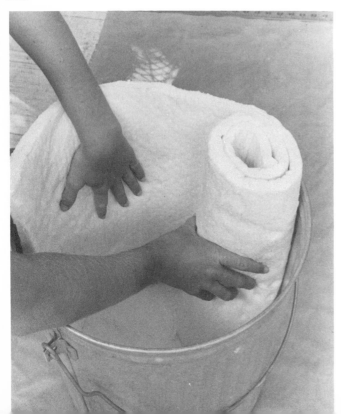

If sufficient material is available, place another disk of ceramic-fiber into the bottom of the container to afford double insulation against the excessive heat of the incoming flame in the firebox area.

At the time of installation, the burner port hole remains covered by the blanket. It will be cut out later, when the burner is fit into the burner port.

The lid of the kiln must be insulated so as to prevent metal surfaces from being exposed to direct heat during operation. Coat the inside of the lid with a heavy application of high temperature glue—sodium silicate liquid or ceramic-fiber liquid cement—and insert a disk of blanket material into the lid, totally covering the flue opening in the same operation. A snug fit of the blanket against the inner wall of the lid will help assure a secure seating. After the lining is secure, make two cross cuts through the blanket at the flue opening. (Fig. 5–10.) Next, gently pull up each triangular piece of blanket and fold it away from the cut onto the outside of the lid. Paint adhesive on the opening perimeter around the flue, and press the four pieces of blanket down firmly, holding them until they remain in place.

If the lid does not already have two outside handles located on its rim, you will have to attach them. Self-tapping sheet metal screws can be used to attach the two outside handles. The lid must be able to be lifted off of the heat chamber body without obstructing the flue opening.

5–10. Two cross cuts are made through the ceramic-fiber blanket to create the flue opening.

The Burner

This kiln's burner, which is designed to inject the maximum amount of heat in the shortest period of time, is of necessity a forced air system. (Fig. 5–11.) This provides a rich mixture of fuel to be forcefully driven, since the amount of air is controlled to achieve correct combustion and maximum B.t.u. (See ch. 1.) The mechanics of the forced air system depend on a used hand-vacuum cleaner, which is placed with the exhaust end directed into the kiln chamber.

A 14″ length of 2″-diam. galvanized or black iron pipe serves well as the burner. Two-thirds of the distance from one end of the pipe, drill a ⅜″ hole directly downward and then, with the drill-bit still turning, angle backward to create an oblong oval hole. This hole provides an opening for insertion of a ⅜″ copper tubing, 8″ long. Cut the tube and check to see that the inside is smooth, with no rough edges or burrs. A small rattail file can be inserted into the tube to clean off any rough areas inside the opening. Next, bend the copper tube by hand in the shape of a gentle "S." (See Fig. 5–11.) Place the tube into the hole in the top of the 2″ pipe so that the front end of the tube is located directly in the center of the pipe and approximately 8″ from the front end. (Note that the inside opening of the copper tube serves as the orifice.) The tube now functions as the fuel line, and it is now brazed to the top of the pipe at its entry point. The brazing joint must completely seal the entry so as not to allow any air or flame to back up at this location during operation. If brazing is not possible, you can seal the tube with a small amount of molten lead.

Connection of the gas line from the burner to the fuel tank is done with a two-foot length of clear plastic tubing. Slip the tubing over the open end of the copper tube extending out of the burner pipe. The dimension inside the plastic tube should be ⅜″ in order for it to slip snuggly over the burner fitting.

The most portable and adaptable vacuum cleaner is a small hand-held one such as a Singer, but if such a device is not available, any type of vacuum cleaner can be used as the source of forced air—from a torpedo-style vac to an upright carpet-sweeper type. The draw hose of a vacuum can be reversed and placed into the back end of the burner pipe to convert the vacuum into a blower. You must be able to cover and uncover the intake end of the vacuum during operation.

When adapting the 2″ burner pipe for fitting onto the vacuum blower output end, it is usually necessary to modify this pipe for a secure, airtight connection. Many hand vacuums have the dirt-collecting bag attached by means of a bayonet clip device. This collecting bag can be removed from the retaining ring clip and the clip fitted onto a collar at the rear end of the burner pipe. (See Fig. 5–11.) This type of vacuum locking arrangement provides a secure, leak-proof fit and is also useful for assembling and disassembling the burner as needed.

When this particular arrangement of vacuum equipment is not available, other devices can be adapted from conventional floor vacuums to achieve the same result.

Fuel Tank and Diaphragm Pressure Gauge

Natural or liquid petroleum gas from any size system can be the fuel source for this kiln. What makes this kiln truly portable, however, is its small 20-lb. LP tank, such as is used for mobile trailers. Filled to capacity, this tank furnishes substantial B.t.u. with strong pressure and can be lifted easily for use on location. A small regulator screwed into the tank connecting valve will control the line pressure during operation and assure that fuel is being expelled at a steady rate. It is necessary, however, to make an adaptor on the tank regulator in order to attach the flexible ⅜″ plastic tubing. A short 4″ piece of ⅜″-diameter copper tubing is flanged and a brass fitting nut attached onto the tank regulator adaptor plug. (Fig. 5–12.)

5–11.

Forced Air Burner

After completing this hookup to the regulator, you can slip the plastic ⅜″ tubing over the copper extension tube, thus connecting the burner to the fuel source. The tank regulator can be set for standard pressure of 11 lbs. per square inch. If a more forceful fuel input is desired, place a high-pressure regulator on the fuel tank. Most high-pressure regulators are designed to pass 15 lbs. per square inch of gas, considerably more fuel than the standard regulator used for home cooking ovens. Local gas service people usually are helpful in advising the proper type of regulator for small tanks which they normally supply and service.

5–12. The tank regulator is fitted with an adaptor for attaching the flexible gas line.

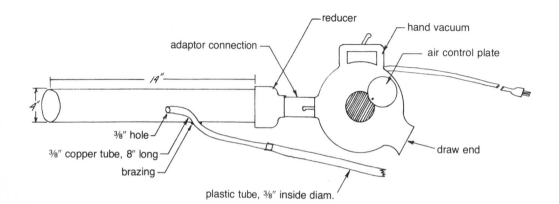

reducer

adaptor connection

hand vacuum

air control plate

14″

4″

⅜″ hole

⅜″ copper tube, 8″ long

brazing

draw end

plastic tube, ⅜″ inside diam.

Flame Baffle System

The fuel input system for the portable raku kiln has a design similar to that of a rapid heat-up metal melting furnace. In both devices, the forced air flame sets up a circular swirling motion of flame around the kiln's lower inner chamber. If you place a raku vessel in the midst of this flame activity, an immediate scorching and blistering of the glazes will occur, due to the flame striking the surface of the vessel without giving the clay body underneath an opportunity to receive a thorough heat saturation first. The glaze surface has reached temperature almost immediately. In order to prevent this type of superficial heating, place the raku vessel above contact with the incoming flame.

First, place two halves of hard refractory bricks, 4″ x 4″ x 2½″, into the bottom of the kiln in order to elevate the raku vessel and keep it away from direct contact with the flame. (See Fig. 5–5.) The lower area of the kiln can now act as the heat-generating firebox, allowing the combustion of the flame within the kiln to take its own natural course and, in turn, expel heat into the upper chamber where the raku vessel is. The object is to keep the ware from direct contact with the incoming flame and allow the remainder of the heat in the chamber to saturate the body of the vessel and melt the glazes. The refractory brick "pedestal" is saturated with heat after several firings, thus assisting the firing process by reflecting heat into the bottom of the raku vessel, an area where it is often difficult for glazes to melt in most conventional raku kilns.

During operation of the kiln, there may be occasions when the raku vessel requires additional protection from flame impingement other than that provided by simply elevating the piece above the incoming flame. Two approaches can be taken for extra protection. A clay sagger can be placed upon the baffle pedestal on which the raku vessel is placed. This sagger can be a deep rectangular bisqued bowl which acts as an encompassing baffle against direct flame contact on the raku vessel. Or else, broken kiln shelf pieces or pieces of brick can be placed around the area where the raku vessel will be during firing. Remember that this kind of baffling will also prevent heat from reaching the raku vessel as quickly as usual, and, therefore, the glaze melting period will take longer than usual.

Firing Procedure

Before igniting this kiln, place the raku vessel on top of the firebox baffle brick pedestal. Return the lid to its original position prior to lighting the kiln. To begin heating the kiln, the air intake hole to the vacuum cleaner blower must be covered with a piece of stiff cardboard. (Fig. 5–13.) Turn the blower on. The blower will continue to operate, but no air will pass into the burner pipe. Next, place a flaming piece of paper into the kiln chamber in front of the burner. The gas tank valve may now be cracked open, allowing gas to flow into the bottom of the kiln chamber. The flaming paper will ignite the fuel and create a long, flowing yellow flame which should appear out of the top of the flue opening. This flame will appear soft and wavy when not mixed with forced air. Increase the gas input at this time to allow a much larger amount of fuel to enter the kiln chamber and the flame to become forceful. Now slowly withdraw the air intake covering and allow the air to be driven into the burner pipe so that it mixes with the flame already in motion. Immediately, the long yellow waving flame will become a forceful hard-driving flame, filling the kiln chamber with extremely high heat.

5–13. The air intake of the vacuum cleaner blower is covered with a stiff piece of cardboard to regulate the combustion of the flame.

During the ignition of this kiln, the following two things will occur. When the air intake cover is pulled back and forced air first introduced into the burner pipe, there will often be a short delay—maybe only half a second—before the fuel and air combine. When combustion does occur, usually a sudden "pop" is heard. The second thing that happens, after the air-fuel mixture is in action is that a low, muffled vibrating sound will be heard—the combination of the forced air and ignited fuel being driven into the kiln chamber. The proper adjustment for this air-fuel combination is at the point when the vibrating sound is at its loudest. At any given fuel input setting (when gas is being allowed into the burner), there is a position for air input which determines the maximum efficiency of fuel-air mixture and the correct combustion level. To determine this point, you can open the air intake cover wider, allowing more air to be forced into the burner pipe, or close the cover down more, allowing less air to be forced into the burner pipe, until the loudest reverberating sound is reached. From the beginning, when more air is mixed with the fuel, the reverberating sound becomes louder and louder, but this continues only up to a certain peak. Past this peak, as more air is allowed through the burner, the sound begins to lessen. The burner is at its maximum efficiency just before this point. It is not always easy to identify the right point when you operate a forced air burner system of this nature. The difference in sound between maximum and near-maximum position is very subtle, and it may take a lot of practice to recognize the exact setting on the air intake cover.

Some vacuum cleaners do not have a strong enough motor to provide sufficient forced air for the kind of adjustments that have been described. With the air intake cover wide open, or even removed, a peak sound of reverberation cannot be reached. However, it may be that sufficient heat is being generated even though fuel efficiency is not at its best level.

After making the proper air/fuel adjustment, be sure that all combustion is contained within the kiln chamber. If flame appears out of the flue opening, it must be trimmed back within the kiln by simply shutting down on the fuel input, readjusting the air intake, and letting the flame react to the new settings. If there is an oxidizing flame (one containing too much air), you can open the fuel valve slightly until a flame appears out of the flue opening. Using this as your reference point, you can trim the flame back again until it remains under the lid of the kiln. This

type of adjustment will assure that heat input is kept up to the maximum space allowed within the kiln chamber.

It is important to understand thoroughly the principle of combustion on this system in order to make it work properly and easily. (Review ch. 1.) The adjustments described for setting the right fuel, air, and combustion take only seconds.

A forced air burner system develops an enormous amount of B.t.u. almost instantaneously—in three to five seconds. Raku temperatures of 1,800 to 2,000°F. are readily available in this time span. Since the clay body of the raku vessel is, in effect, a refractory insulating material, it will take a few minutes for it to catch up with the heat of the kiln chamber. Meanwhile, if the glaze has been applied thickly, the raku vessel will initially react to the sudden exposure to heat by blistering, bubbling, and finally erupting until the glaze is a smooth flowing cover upon the face of the vessel. If the glaze has been applied relatively thinly, its flow on the vessel surface will appear normal, as with any glaze in the melting process.

To remove the raku vessel from the kiln chamber, simply shut off the kiln, remove the lid, and lift the vessel out with a pair of metal tongs. Then treat the vessel in organic matter and water, as described earlier in this chapter.

Assembly

The portable raku kiln can be assembled for use in the following manner: Attach the vacuum cleaner blower system to the back end of the burner; place the burner into position in the burner port on the bottom lower side of the kiln container, and plug the blower in. If necessary, prop the rear of the burner up off the floor so that the front will be level when inside the kiln. As already mentioned the burner should fit snugly into the burner port so as *not* to allow a backing out of flame during operation. Attach the flexible plastic tubing to the back end of the copper fuel injection tube extending out of the rear of the burner. Attach the other end of this tube to the regulator diaphragm on the gas tank. Move the tank with the tube attached as far as possible from the kiln. (Fig. 5–14.) The entire system is now ready for operation.

5–14. Extend the gas tank away from the operating kiln.

Materials List for the Portable Raku Kiln
Kiln container:
One 10-gallon galvanized garbage can

Thermal blanket:
2300°F. ceramic-fiber blanket, ½″ thick, 6 lb. density (43″ x 18″, can lining only)
Lid lining: 16″ diam. disk
Base lining (inside floor): 2 pieces, 12¼ diam. disk
Total blanket requirements: 9 sq. ft.

Adhesive:
1 pint high-temperature ceramic-fiber liquid cement or liquid sodium-silicate

Burner system (see Fig. 5–11):
1 piece 2″ x 14″ black iron or galvanized pipe (no threads)
1 piece ⅜″ x 8″ copper tubing
1 piece ⅜″ I.D. x 36″ flexible tubing (clear plastic or other)
1 reducer adaptor ring, from 2″ to suit vac attachment

Forced air system:
1 used vacuum cleaner (preferably hand-held type, but torpedo or other type is sufficient)

Fuel tank:
1 portable LPG 20-gallon with high-pressure regulator

Regulator attachment (see photo 5–12):
One 4″ x ⅜″ O.D. copper tube, flanged on one end
One ⅜″ brass flange nut (slides over copper tube)
One ½″ O.D. to ⅜″ brass reducer (fits into regulator and flange nut)

No damper shelf required

6. Production Kiln with Two Car Beds

6–1. Seventy-cubic-foot production kiln.

The seventy-cubic-foot kiln discussed in this chapter was built in Oaxaca, Mexico, for firing handmade production pottery and was constructed without firebrick of any sort. (Fig. 6–1.) Shortages of conventional refractory bricks prevented construction of this kiln at the scheduled time. With delivery of bricks being delayed for nine to twelve months, an alternative kiln design was needed so that construction could get underway. The new materials described in this book were available on call in Mexico since they are kept in stock for many industrial heat applications. Also available were the necessary steel products for making the kiln frame, as well as standard casting refractory materials for the two roll-in car beds. Therefore, a brickless kiln was designed and built.

This kiln is designed to shuttle two car beds, alternately, through the heat chamber on a continuous schedule. While one car bed, loaded with pottery, is in the kiln being fired, the second is outside being stacked. It can then be rolled into the kiln when the fired car bed comes out. This procedure assures maximum efficiency of production. To maintain the greatest flexibility of movement, two counterweighted guillotine doors with pressure locking clamps are provided. The lightweight ceramic-fiber blanket and backup mineral wool block make it possible for one person to raise and lower the kiln doors easily.

This kiln operates on the updraft principle of heat movement, which makes for ease in construction and simplicity of function. Ten upright cast-iron commercial burners, operating on LPG, are installed in the center of the kiln floor. (Fig. 6–2.) The kiln's temperature objective is to cone one (2077°F.)—high enough to eliminate all lead-based glazes and to provide a strong vitrified clay body at a reasonably low cost.

The inside of the kiln and the two doors are lined with a 2,300°F. insulating ceramic-fiber blanket, backed by a 3″ mineral wool block having a heat tolerance of 1,800°F. (Should higher temperatures be desired, install a 2,600°F. blanket.) The mineral wool block absorbs heat from the exterior face of the blanket and acts as a structural support upon which the blanket is pinned. It is held in position by an angle iron frame 2″ wide. Construct the frame first, and fit the block into it, rather than the reverse. Even during its first firing, this kiln showed excellent results: Heat was relatively even, the kiln atmosphere clean (twice the flue opening capacity is provided), and the ceramic-fiber materials functioned superbly.

6–2. This kiln has ten upright cast-iron commercial burners in the center of the kiln floor.

Kiln Shelves

The initial design of any large kiln is best calculated around the size of its ware-stacking shelves. In many cases, shelves must be special ordered, which can take several weeks or even months. However, you need not await shelf delivery; construction can begin as soon as you know the size of the shelves. Indeed, because of delivery problems, the first test firings on the Oaxaca kiln had to be conducted using mullite shelves, even though the design called for silicon-carbide shelves measuring 15″ x 13″ by 1″ thick. These dimensions allowed four shelves to be placed next to each other on their 15″ side, thus covering a total area of 60″ in length. The car bed is 67″ overall, which makes for a leeway of approximately 7″

between it and each set of shelves. (Fig. 6–3.) If placed on their 13″ side, in pairs, the shelves would take a space of 26″. If you left a 1″ gap in the center between the shelves, the area would be 27″ overall. The car bed width and the width of the kiln inside is 28″, providing for an area of passage when the bed is rolled into the kiln. (Fig. 6–4.)

The position of the burner ports in the car beds requires that the bottom set of shelves be placed directly over these openings in order to baffle the flame and protect the pottery stacked above. In addition, it is often necessary to place a double set of bottom shelves—one on top of the other with a small ¾″-spacer in between—over the burner ports so that the lower ware stacking area does not receive excessive heat. Placement of shelves at upper levels should be such that heat is circulated throughout the kiln stacking chamber to provide even saturation. (This subject is discussed further at the end of the chapter under the heading "Firing Procedure.")

6–3.

Roll-In Car Bed—Top View

All dimensions are on center of holes.
Holes are ⅜″ diam.

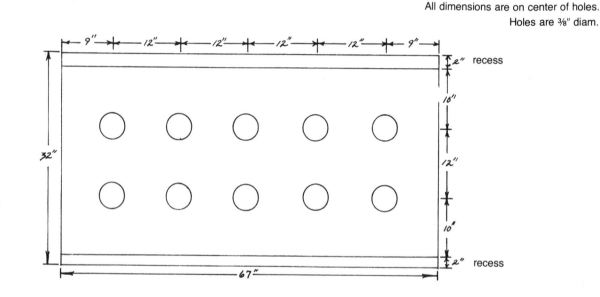

6–4.

Roll-In Car Bed

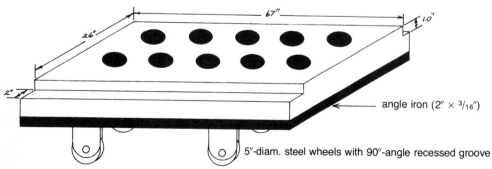

angle iron (2″ × ³/₁₆″)

5″-diam. steel wheels with 90°-angle recessed groove

Track and Frame

The two car beds require a 3″ angle iron track laid down on two cemented building brick walls 16′ long. These walls rise 4″ from the floor surface. The angle iron bars are placed in an inverted position, raising the tracks an additional 3″. Placing the track above floor level provides additional height for the burners. (Fig. 6–5.)

Level the angle iron track and then embed it in concrete on top of the brick wall. Now secure the angle iron permanently so there is no possibility of shifting when the cast refractory car beds, heavy with shelves and pottery, are in operation. The track must be absolutely level and at an exact 30″ width from top center to top center all the way because if there is a difference in track width, the grooved wheels will bind and inhibit movement of the car beds.

These beds must be able to roll smoothly because of the load they carry.

Mark the midpoint of the 16′ track and measure a steel angle iron frame for the kiln chamber in accordance with this point. The frame measures 67″ long by 55″ high by 36″ wide. (See Fig. 6–5.) First weld the two side panel frames together including four vertical ribs which support a thin sheet of tin. (Fig. 6–6.) This becomes an exterior protective covering for the mineral block which will be set into the frame. Place the two side panels upright, opposite each other, and clamp an angle iron cross member in position to hold the panels while you level the entire structure for absolute plumb. (Fig. 6–7.) After checking all angles for square, you can weld the entire kiln frame.

6–5.

Updraft Roll-In Car Bed Kiln—End View

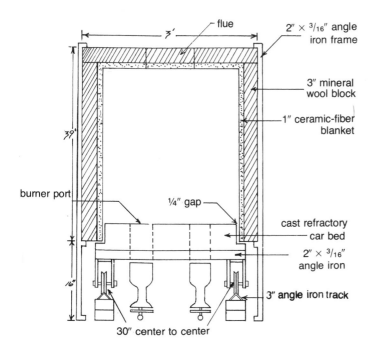

6–6. Two side panel frames are welded to include four tee iron ribs which will support a panel of sheet tin.

6–7. The side panels are set up over the track and clamped in position for leveling and welding.

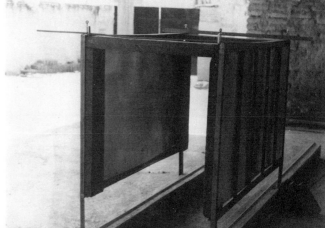

Mineral Block and Ceramic-Fiber Installation

Once the completed kiln frame is in place, with sheet tin inserted into the side panels, you can insert the mineral block forms. Each mineral wool block measures 36″ long by 6″ wide and is 3″ thick. The iron frame has a ledge 16″ from the floor along the bottom of each side panel, and this 2″-wide ledge supports the mineral wool blocks vertically along the kiln's inside wall. There is a 3″ allowance above the vertical mineral block on which the horizontal blocks will be placed to make up the kiln's inside ceiling.

Place all mineral wool blocks to be used in the kiln ceiling together on the floor and indicate the flue openings on the block face with a soft pencil. Space four 8″ x 4″ flue openings evenly across the length of the ceiling block so that one-half of each opening is located on the outside edge of each block. Cut the block with a small coping saw; although firm, the material is relatively easy to cut. (Fig. 6–8.) After you have cut out the flue openings, drive a 3/8″ cold-roll round iron, 35½″ long, into the center of each block for support of the mineral wool.

Construction begins when you insert one 3′ block on each side panel and then one across the top into the kiln angle iron frame. Continue this sequence, from side to side and across the top, until the entire kiln frame is completed. Keep in mind that only those blocks serving as ceiling support contain a round iron.

Cut 1″-thick ceramic-fiber blanket, 102″ long to cover both sides and ceiling continuously without a seam. Blanket widths are cut so as to prevent seams falling at the same location as mineral block seams. Before pinning the blanket to the mineral wool block, apply ceramic-fiber liquid cement to ceiling joints. If other gaps appear on the surface of the block, caulk them first with small scraps of ceramic-fiber blanket and then fill them in or cover them with ceramic-fiber liquid cement.

Bend a number of U-shaped Nichrome wire pins to secure the blanket to the mineral wool block. You will need several hundred of these pins to fasten the entire area of the kiln chamber as well as the guillotine doors. One person holds the blanket while a second person punctures the blanket and secures the pin into the backing block. (Figs. 6–9, 6–10, and 6–11.) After enough pins have been inserted to let loose of the blanket safely, continue additional pinning approximately every 3″ over the kiln's entire surface. Although the blanket has not yet been cut through the flue openings, pinning is done at that location also. Do the final pinning through the body of the

block and through the outside tin covering. Tie the wire together outside the kiln to insure permanent placement of the blanket. Now cut the flue openings through to the block opening. Coat the edges with ceramic-fiber liquid cement. Finally, spray the entire surface of the interior kiln lining with a liquid rigidizer. (Fig. 6–12.)

6–8. Flue openings measuring 8″ x 4″ are cut out of the mineral block with a coping saw.

Roll-In Car Beds

The two car beds are constructed from dense refractory casting mix in order to provide a substantially rigid and strong body for carrying the payload of shelves and pottery. You can purchase this material from a foundry supply source. Make a wooden form that includes a pair of 2″ recessed ledges in the casting. (See Fig. 6–3.) Situated

6–9. A length of ceramic-fiber blanket measuring 102″ has been cut for pinning up against the mineral wool block.

6–10. The blanket is held in position prior to pinning it into the mineral wool block backing.

6–11. Nichrome wires bent into a U shape secure the ceramic-fiber blanket to the mineral wool block.

6–12. All ceramic-fiber blanket surfaces are sprayed with a liquid rigidizer.

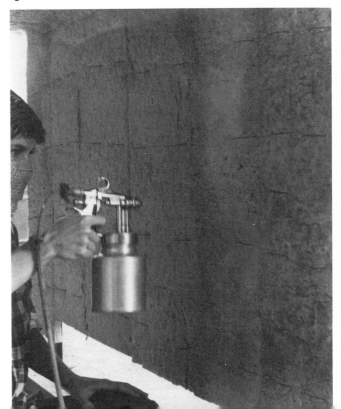

one on each side of the bed, these ledges ride under the bottom lip of the ceramic-fiber blanket wall inside the kiln and become the "heat seal" which prevents heat from escaping along the kiln floor's bottom edge during operation. (Fig. 6–13.) Each bed measures 30″ in overall width. The 2″ recess—1″ below the surface on either side of the bed—leaves a 26″ raised surface. The length of the car beds is 67″, the same as the kiln frame; the inside measurements of each car bed frame measure 67″ x 30″ x 4″.

In order to provide for a recessed ledge during the casting of the car beds, make a wooden frame consisting of two boards measuring 2″ x 1″ x 67″ on the floor of the frame. Each car bed is actually cast upside down. During casting, make ten burner ports by positioning round cartons or bottles in two rows 8″ from the inside edge of the bed. (See Fig. 6–3.) The burner ports in each car bed must be in the exact same place: Both car beds use the same set of burners, so burner ports must align properly.

After the casting mix has cured and the mold frame has been removed, weld a 2″ x $3/16$″ angle iron frame securely around the casting to carry the weight of the bed, which will be approximately 600 lbs. On the bottom of the iron frame, measure lines exactly 30″ apart. Attach the four steel grooved wheels on this line so that the center of the wheel groove matches the 30″ line. (Fig. 6–14.) Each wheel must be on the true center line at 30″ widths so it will match the top of the angle iron track running through the kiln. For best support, attach the wheels 18″ in from the end of the bed frame.

After it is completed, lift each bed and turn it over onto the kiln track. (Fig. 6–15.) The beds can be rolled into the kiln's interior to check for fitting. (See Fig. 6–13.) If the ceramic-fiber blanket interferes with the car bed's recessed ledge, the bed can be gently moved in and out of the kiln to cut its own seating against the blanket and thus assure the tight position of the car bed heat seal in relation to the ceramic-fiber wall. If the ceramic-fiber wall is slightly receded from the ledge of the car bed, you can pull it away from the mineral wool block backing and place a thin strip of additional ceramic-fiber material behind it as a shim. The blanket can then be pinned back against the mineral wool block to secure it again. Once you have achieved absolute seating of the bed ledge and blanket, you can coat this blanket location with rigidizer and then paint it with ceramic-fiber liquid cement to give the blanket a substantially hardened surface at a point where there will be constant movement.

78

6–13. The outside recessed ledge of the car bed rides under the bottom lip of the ceramic-fiber blanket wall.

6–14. The four steel wheels are mounted upon the car bed frame at exactly 30″ from wheel center on one side across to the opposite side.

6–15. The completed car bed is turned over onto the kiln track.

Guillotine Doors and Door Track

This kiln has two guillotine doors—one at each end—to make movement of the two car beds possible. One door opens and a car bed of pottery is rolled in to be fired; later, after the first car bed has been rolled back out, the opposite door will be opened to allow entry and firing at the second car bed. Each door rises above the top of the kiln by means of riding up a tilted iron frame track. A counterweight attached to each door makes movement upon the track possible without lifting the entire weight of the door. During operation, three compression locking clamps keep the doors sealed against the kiln.

The doors are constructed of two angle iron frames measuring 36″ x 38″ with seven oversized ⅜″ holes on each 38″-length side. These holes are located at the center of each block which will be inserted in the frame. Place a sheet of tin into the frame as a protection against exterior damage to the mineral wool block backing. Put six mineral wool blocks—each measuring 36″ x 6″ x 3″—together face up on the floor, and add one more piece measuring 36″ x 2″ x 3″, cutting this narrow 2″ piece from a full-size 3″-wide block. Indicate three peepholes, each 2¼″ square, on the block, spacing them evenly, so that one-half of each opening is marked into the side of the block. Cut these holes from the block in the same fashion as you did the flue openings. (Fig. 6–16.) Make plugs for the holes for mineral wool block and then coat the plugs with ceramic-fiber liquid cement. (Fig. 6–17.) Insert all blocks into the door frame, and hammer a ⅜″ round iron, 36⅜″ long, through the center of each block from outside the iron frame. Take care not to drive the iron through the peep opening. (Fig. 6–18.) After seating, the ends of the round iron should be resting in the angle iron hole on both sides of the block. This anchors the block against the door frame so that the block will not fall forward when in position on the door frame track.

You can now pin ceramic-fiber blanket on the mineral wool block in the same manner as was done for the inner wall of the kiln. It is advisable, however, to anchor the blanket after the door has been placed on the suspension track and the pulley and counterweight system have been attached. The blanket in front of the kiln opening measures 34″ x 40″, it need not be extended to the outside edges of the door frame.

Weld together two angle iron frames, open at one end, to serve as the door track where the door will ride above the kiln. Each frame, made from 1½″ angle iron, mea-

6–16. Peepholes for the doors are cut halfway into each block of mineral wool.

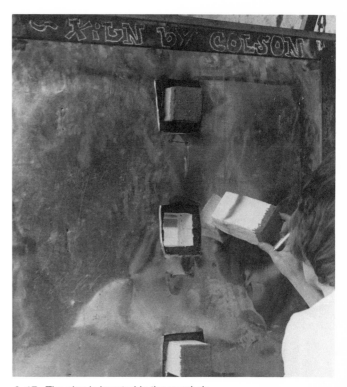

6–17. The plug is inserted in the peephole.

6–18. A length of ⅜″ round iron is driven into each mineral wool block for additional support.

sures seven feet long. The track width inside is 37", one inch wider than the door frame itself, allowing ½" play so the door will not bind as it goes up and down the track. Secure two horizontal pieces of angle iron, 10" long, on the bottom leg of the kiln frame on each side. These pieces extend forward 5" and act as stops for the door at the lowered position of the kiln opening. (Fig. 6–19.)

Before installing the track frame, the door should be placed in position, resting on the lower horizontal stops and butted up against the kiln opening. Next, place the track frame outside the door frame 10" away from the outside top edge of the front of the kiln. (See Fig. 6–19.) The track frame should be checked carefully for alignment, squared, trued, and clamped solidly into position. Secure two supporting struts at an angle to each track frame from the top of the kiln to help hold the frame firmly above the kiln when the door rides upward. (Fig. 6–20.) Weld or bolt securely the entire door assembly at both ends of the kiln. (Fig. 6–21.)

The door is now ready for hanging and counterbalancing. Place two metal loops at the top of the outside of the door frame 2" from each corner. Put two more open loops at the top of the track frame 2" from each corner. Hang two

pulleys with ¼" grooved metal wheels from the top loops of the track frame, and then connect each door with two ¼" stainless steel twisted cables, 7' long. (Fig. 6–22.) Draw one end of the cables up through the door loops and bolt it securely with small U bolts which span the doubled-up cable at this point. String the remaining cable through the pulleys above and secure it to a counterweight. (See Fig. 6–23.)

The counterweight can be any device heavy enough to float the door up and down the track easily. (Fig. 6–23.) It should not draw the door up by itself when the door is in position to lock into the kiln opening. Each counterweight should be approximately 20 lbs., giving each door a total counterweight load of 40 lbs. This amount will vary in other kilns of this design since the iron materials making up the door frame could be heavier or lighter. You can use a stack of bricks, sandbags, a chunk of railroad track, or simply a cluster of discarded auto parts for the counterweight (see Fig. 6–2), but it is helpful not to have the material measure larger than 6" wide or 20" long or it may become an obstruction when you roll the car bed into the kiln.

6–19.
Door Track and Door Assembly

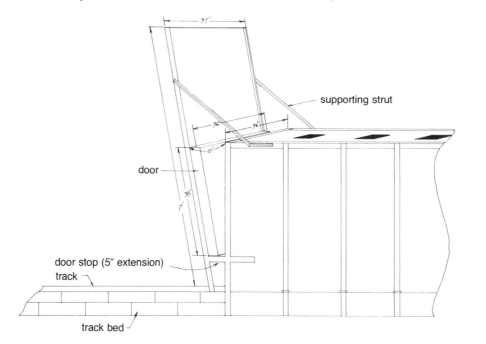

6–20. Supporting struts for the door track are welded to the frame of the kiln.

6–22. Each door is connected to the guiding track with steel cables which run through pulleys.

6–21. The entire door assembly on both ends of the kiln is bolted or welded securely in position.

6–23. Counterweights must be adjusted to allow the door to ride up and down the track with ease.

Door-Locking Clamps

Each door has three locking pressure clamps which secure it snugly into a heat-sealed position against the kiln opening. The clamp is made up of one moving and one stable component. Figure 6–24 shows the clamp in the locked position, and Figure 6–25 the clamp mounted on top of the kiln frame in the open position.

Note in Figures 6–26 and 6–27 how the offset ¼" bolt of the locking hook is placed ½" from the mounting bolt. Once you pull the draw arm down, the door is pulled forward approximately 1". After the door is resting at the bottom of the door track, it must be pushed forward manually about 4" until the locking hook can be engaged over the matching tongue on the door. (Fig. 6–28.) It is advisable—when the door is in position—to place all three locking hooks over the matching tongues on the door frame before you pull down on the draw arm. In this way, the door will remain relatively loose and can be adjusted slightly before drawing it tightly into place against the abutting kiln opening.

During first-time fittings, you will find it helpful to lock one door, enter the kiln, and check the seating of the ceramic-fiber seams from inside. The compressed locking clamps should provide a totally gap-free seal. The ceramic-fiber blanket inside the door should not be coated with a rigidizer but rather left pliable during the door-fitting operation. You can do the rigidizing later, when you are sure that each door seats properly and consistently. Should constant compression of the blanket cause a loosening of the locking position, you can glue an additional strip of blanket and pin it across the end face of the mineral wool block on the kiln opening.

6–24. The door-locking clamp in the closed position.

6–25. The door-locking clamp in the open position above the kiln opening.

Elevation View of Locking Assembly Mounted on Typical Kiln

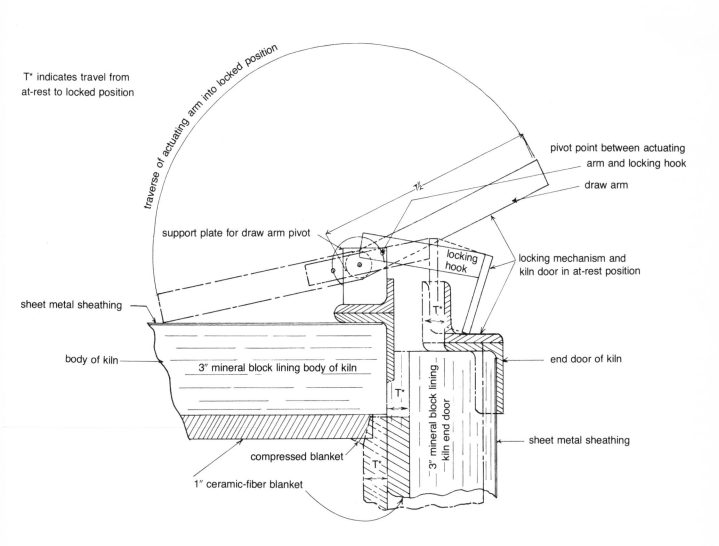

T* indicates travel from
at-rest to locked position

traverse of actuating arm into locked position

pivot point between actuating
arm and locking hook

draw arm

1½

support plate for draw arm pivot

locking
hook

locking mechanism and
kiln door in at-rest position

sheet metal sheathing

end door of kiln

body of kiln

3″ mineral block lining body of kiln

3″ mineral block lining
kiln end door

sheet metal sheathing

T*

T*

T*

compressed blanket

1″ ceramic-fiber blanket

locking assembly designed by William Sheppard

Plan View of Locking Assembly in Locked Position

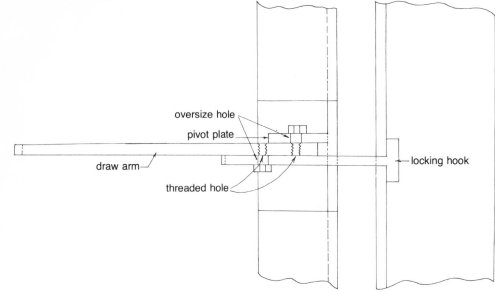

oversize hole

pivot plate

draw arm

threaded hole

locking hook

6–28. The kiln door being pushed forward manually.

Burners

This kiln requires ten simple cast-iron atmospheric commercial burners, which are mounted vertically on two separate manifold lines. (Fig. 6–29.) Each manifold has a separate controlling valve. When a car bed is inside a kiln, one set of five burners is located in dead center of every other burner port while the other set of five burners is in dead center of the alternating burner ports. The two sets of burners should be marked Set A and Set B to identify which burners are on the same manifold line at the time of ignition.

Because of the complication of manifold design and installation, it is best to have a professional gas service company make the burner installation. Each burner must be situated directly under its burner ports when each car bed is in place, so that flame will not strike the underside of the bed. The top of each burner should be only ¼″ below the underside of the car bed. During installation, move each of the car beds in position inside the kiln to check alignment of all the burner ports with the burners. If there is any question, roll one of the car beds into the kiln and get inside to check all alignments. Each burner should provide a total output of 21,000 B.t.u. for firing the kiln to cone ten. Considerably less B.t.u. per burner are required if the kiln is fired at a lower temperature. If LPG is the fuel supply, a No. 54 orifice drill will provide 21,200 B.t.u. for propane; with natural gas as the source of fuel, a No. 49 orifice drill will provide 20,100 B.t.u. Be certain that all ten burners have the same size orifice, since size differences will result in an inconsistent flame configuration, which will in turn affect the firing.

6–29. Ten simple cast-iron atmospheric commercial burners are installed in the floor of the kiln.

Damper Control Shelves

The four flue openings cut into the roof of the kiln provide nearly double the necessary allowance for heat release. You control the flues by means of dampers made of four ½"-thick pieces of mullite shelves cut to the size of 12" x 5". Each shelf has a 1" slot, 1" from one end. (The slot is made by boring a series of ¼" holes with a masonory bit. Each hole runs into the adjacent hole to create the slot.) Bend a piece of flat iron, ½" x ⅛" x 12", with a right angle on one end and a loop at the other end to serve as a handle. When you place this damper lever into the damper slot, it enables you to push the damper closed or pull it open. To guide the damper, screw two pieces of flat iron, ½" x ⅛" x 35", across the top of the kiln on either side of each flue opening. Braze a similar piece of flat iron, ½" x ⅛" x 5½", at the end of the damper guides to serve as a stop, beyond which the damper shelf cannot go. Small white marks on these track guides indicate the half, three-quarter, and other positions of the damper shelf over the flue opening. Figure 6–30 shows two of the dampers over the flue openings.

It may be necessary to cut a portion of the protective tin covering away from the flue opening, to allow the damper shelf to slide without hanging up. The mineral wool block surface on which the damper will move is coated with ceramic-fiber liquid cement, and this cement should be allowed to harden so as to protect the surface of the mineral wool block under the damper shelf. Number each damper one through four for identification purposes when you refer to firing procedures and charts.

Firing Procedure

The position of the burner ports in the car beds allows flame to come directly up through the floor, and it is therefore necessary to divert this flame through the kiln in such a manner as to create the best heat effect. Shelf stacking is an important factor in influencing the way flame moves through the kiln. Place the first layer of shelves directly over all burner ports. This area—from the car bed floor to the underside of the first shelves—actually constitutes the firebox. Note in Figure 6–31 that a gap is left in the center of the first course of shelves in order to force the flame to move up into the center of the kiln, as well as out along the outside of it. From this lowest point upward, the position of the shelves alternates, from course to course, so that heat is then required to move up through the center of the stacking chamber from gap to gap. In effect, this holds

6–30. Damper shelves are guided by two metal flat-iron tracks above the flue openings.

6–31. Stacking is arranged so as to leave a gap at alternating levels for flame circulation.

heat in the kiln longer, and makes it circulate thoroughly throughout the ware before it escapes out of the flue openings above.

If the firebox area becomes too hot and tends to overheat pottery on the lower shelves, you would do well to arrange a double set of shelves, as described earlier in the chapter. But although the double-shelf system helps to take the brunt of the direct flame, it does not, however, necessarily resolve problems that may arise due to uneven heat saturation. Saturation is controlled by the manner in which the kiln is fired.

After a loaded car bed is placed into the kiln and the guillotine doors are locked into position, one set of five burners should be turned on low. (In this case, "low" means that the flame should extend no further than the opening gaps of the first set of shelves.) Keep this flame length for one and a half to two hours. Next, turn the same five burners up slightly, enough to bring the flame up in between the shelf gaps in the center of the kiln chamber, and keep this flame for an additional hour. During this time, hold as much heat as possible in the kiln by closing the dampers two-thirds. After three additional hours, ignite the second set of five burners and bring them up to approximately the same flame level as the first operating set. Two hours later the kiln will begin to acquire color—at 1,000°F. or better. As heat increases, you can open the flues slightly to avoid back pressure and premature reduction.

If possible, the total firing cycle should be elongated to at least eight hours. Following the schedule just described, it would not be difficult to reach maximum temperature within six or six and a half hours, but such a short firing cycle will more than likely result in uneven heat, with a hot bottom and a cold top. You can acquire even heat saturation by drawing out the heat cycle at the lower temperature range, between 1,000 and 1,800°F. This affords opportunity for the refractory shelves and the pottery, as well as the car bed, to become saturated with heat and radiate it back into the chamber. Since the ceramic-fiber blanket absorbs almost no heat, it is most important to pay attention to heat soaking the refractory items in the kiln. Keep in mind that during the first firing, a good deal of moisture will be driven out of the cast car bed in the form of steam, and, in addition, there will be smoke from the burning of organic binders in the blanket and mineral wool block. These factors may throw the first firing off slightly, but not enough to make conditions uncontrollable.

After the kiln has reached temperature, care must be taken to control the cooling cycle. Shutting the kiln off completely leaves only the hard refractory materials inside cooling down. The ceramic-fiber insulation will hold only the heat being radiated from the refractory materials in the kiln, and nothing more. It may be necessary to "down fire" the kiln after reaching temperature. However, experience has shown that during cone one firings of this kiln, there was no need to down fire; there was enough heat in the refractory materials to provide a gradual cooling cycle that was sufficiently compatible with the glazes. Cone one, in relationship to cone ten, is a middle-of-the-road temperature between high-fired and low-fired objectives: The higher temperature would probably require down firing.

The suggestions made here are based on actual experience, but do not necessarily mean that the same conditions will develop elsewhere with the same kiln. The fuel used for firing this kiln is a Mexican LPG, which is usually a mixture of unknown gasses. These gases are definitely hotter than natural gas, but their rating compared to standard propane is another thing altogether. If this kiln were fired with natural gas, which is usually rated at about 1,000 B.t.u. per cubic foot, the firing cycle could certainly differ from the one described here.

Although mullite shelves were used in early test firings, silicon-carbide shelves were used with later firings. Silicon-carbide shelves conducted heat better, resulting in more even and better heat saturation in later firings. After the initial firings, positioning of shelves was adjusted slightly; some gaps were closed slightly and others were opened. All of these factors should be taken into account as important variables in firing a kiln.

For production purposes, this kiln is a gem. Its construction takes less time than any conventional brick kiln of its type and size. It is unsurpassed in flexibility of movement for loading and unloading since there is complete freedom to move around the car beds. The kiln's ceramic-fiber insulating composition provides absolutely tight seals and superb heat-containing qualities. This is truly a space-age kiln.

Materials List for the Production Kiln with Two Car Beds

Track:
2 pieces steel angle iron (each 3″ x $^3/_{16}$″ x 16′)

Kiln frame (see Fig. 6–5):
4 pieces steel angle iron (each 2″ x $^3/_{16}$″ x 55″)
4 pieces steel angle iron (each 2″ x $^3/_{16}$″ x 67″)
2 pieces steel angle iron (each 2″ x $^3/_{16}$″ x 36″)
8 pieces steel tee iron (each 1″ x $^1/_8$″ x 42″)
(serve as exterior vertical ribs on side panels)
2 pieces sheet tin (each 67″ x 42″)
(serve as exterior paneling to protect mineral wool block)
4 pieces steel angle iron (each 2″ x $^3/_{16}$″ x 10″)
(serve as lower door stops at kiln opening)
12 pieces $^3/_8$″ x 36½″ cold-roll or stainless
steel round iron
(serve as reinforcing ceiling block)

Guillotine door frame (see also Fig. 6–5):
4 pieces steel angle iron (each 2″ x $^3/_{16}$″ x 36″)
4 pieces steel angle iron (each 2″ x $^3/_{16}$″ x 38″)
6 pieces steel angle iron (each 2″ x $^3/_{16}$″ x 1$^3/_{16}$″)
(serve as door clamp tongues)
2 pieces sheet tin (each 36″ x 38″)
(serve as exterior paneling to protect mineral wool block)
7 pieces $^3/_8$″ x 36″ cold-roll or stainless steel iron
rods (for imbedding into mineral block)
Four ¼″ eye bolts (for securing doors to cable and hanging pulleys)
28′ twisted steel cable, ¼″ diam. (cut to 4 pieces, each 7′)
Sixteen ¼″ cable U-bolts (for fastening cable to door and
door track)
4 counterweights, each approximately 20 lbs. (brick,
sandbag, or steel scrap)

Door tracks:
2 pieces steel angle iron (each 1½″ x $^1/_8$″ x 37″)
4 pieces steel angle iron (each 1½″ x $^1/_8$″ x 84″)
4 pieces steel angle iron (each 1½″ x $^1/_8$″ x 48″) (for supporting struts)
8 pieces steel angle iron (each 1½″ x $^1/_8$″ x 51½″) (used as
cross brace support—see Fig. 6-2)
Four ¼″ eye bolts (for securing doors to cable and hanging pulleys)
4 metal pulleys with ¼″ grooved metal wheels

Car beds (see Figs. 6–3 and 6–4):
Wood casting frame: 2 wood boards (each 4″ x ¾″ x
31½″)
2 wood boards (each 4″ x ¾″ x 67″)
2 wood boards (each 2″ x 1″ x 67″)
Ten 3″ diameter bottles or round cartons (placed in casting mix to form burner ports)

Frame:
4 steel angle iron (each 2″ x $^3/_{16}$″ x 67″)
4 steel angle iron (each 2″ x $^3/_{16}$″ x 30$^3/_8$″)

Wheels:
8 steel, 5½″ diam. with 90° inserted groove, ¾″ deep; rigid
steel frame (each 3″ x ¼″)

Casting mix:
600 lbs. refractory casting mix (See Suppliers List. Follow
manufacturer's instructions for casting.)

Door locking clamps (see Figs. 6–26 and 6–27):
6 pieces 1″ x ¼″ x 7½″ flat iron (serve as draw arm)
6 pieces 2¼″ x 1¼″ x ¼″ flat iron (serve as mounting
plate)
6 pieces 4$^7/_{32}$″ x 1″ x ¼″ flat iron (serve as locking tongue
extension)
6 pieces 1″ x 2¾″ x ¼″ flat iron (serve as locking tongue)
6 pieces 2″ x 2″ x $^3/_{16}$″ angle iron (serve as mount for
clamp assembly)
Twelve ½″ x ¼″ machine bolts
Twelve ¼″ lock washers

Mineral wool block (for entire kiln including doors):
48 pieces 6″ x 3″ x 36″ mineral wool block (Order a few
additional blocks for future repair and other needs.)

Thermal blanket:
Ceramic-fiber blanket, 1″ thick, 6 lb. density
100 sq. ft., 2300°F. rated for low fire operation
100 sq. ft., 2600°F. rated for high fire operation
(This is 30 sq. ft. in excess of exact requirements.)

Ceramic-fiber liquid cement:
One gallon

Liquid rigidizer:
One gallon

Nichrome wire:
One roll, 50′ long. Must be cut into 8″ lengths and bent into U-pins for mounting thermal blanket to mineral wool block.

Dampers:
4 mullite shelves (each 12″ x 5″ x ½″)
1 flat iron (½″ x ⅛″ x 12″) used as damper adjustment handle
8 flat iron (each ½″ x ⅛″ x 35″) used as damper guides
4 flat iron (each ½″ x ⅛″ x 5½″) used as damper guide stops

Burners:
10 cast-iron atmospheric commercial burners

Shelves:
30 silicon-carbide (each 15″ x 13″ x 1″) for one car bed

Posts:
100, made by cutting standard-sized hard refractory bricks lengthwise and again into halves, quarters, and three-quarters, approximately 35 whole bricks needed.

7. The Cast Kiln

The cast kiln described and illustrated in this chapter is a catenary kiln in form. As mentioned in chapter 2, the simplicity of the catenary form eliminates numerous engineering problems. Other kiln forms such as the Roman arch and similar structures with arch thrusts require exterior buttressing or other devices, but the catenary arch form has become a universal kiln structure because it is essentially self-contained.

The cast kiln serves two basic purposes: It provides a means of making a kiln without bricks, and it eliminates the need for a structural retaining shell to hold the insulating material in position, thus cutting down construction to a minimum. A small cast kiln, under ten cubic feet, has the additional attribute of being movable—a characteristic usually not available in brick-constructed kilns.

Preparing the Mix

The size of the catenary cast kiln will depend primarily upon your requirements. If this kiln is for small pieces of pottery, it should be quite a different size than one cast for large pieces, or for a production line of pottery. With this in mind, no specific dimensions have been given for this kiln since the principles of construction are applicable to any given size. The cast kiln size can be the same as that illustrated for the twelve-cubic-foot kiln in chapter 2, or it can be calculated to suit other needed dimensions. (For building the catenary form, see the instructions in ch. 2.) Since the internal area of the catenary form narrows near the top, it is advisable to determine the size of the arch by the size of the shelves in stock. Once the catenary arch

form is built, you can use it over again for constructing or casting additional kilns in the future. For casting, place the arch form, which is made of wood and masonite, arch end down with the bottom open end up. This is the best position for applying the high-temperature mix to be cast within the form. (Fig. 7–1.)

For a small kiln of 10 cubic feet or less, it is best to tamp the casting mix inside the kiln form in the following manner: Block the form in a stable position, open end (bottom) directly up. (Fig. 7–2.) The curved narrow top of the form should rest on a floor or other flat surface with wood blocks or similar material butted up against the arch to prevent tilting during tamping. Make up the insulating mix and place handfuls of the prepared material inside the form, tamping it down with a piece of 2″ x 4″ wood block. Tamp the casting mix until it becomes homogeneous with the mix surrounding it. Continue this method of application for the entire inner surface of the arch form, right up to its exterior opening. Even application—2″ thick—is essential throughout, including at the front and back vertical panels of the form. To assure proper thickness in all areas, you can insert a needle or thin headless nail through the wet mix to the form's surface. When you withdraw the nail or needle, keep a finger there to mark the top of the mix surface and measure the remaining length with a ruler. Spot-check areas in this way during application. Low areas should be built up with more mix until you achieve the proper thickness. After the entire inner surface of the arch form has been covered with casting mix, you can smooth it for a final finish by drawing, or wiping, a

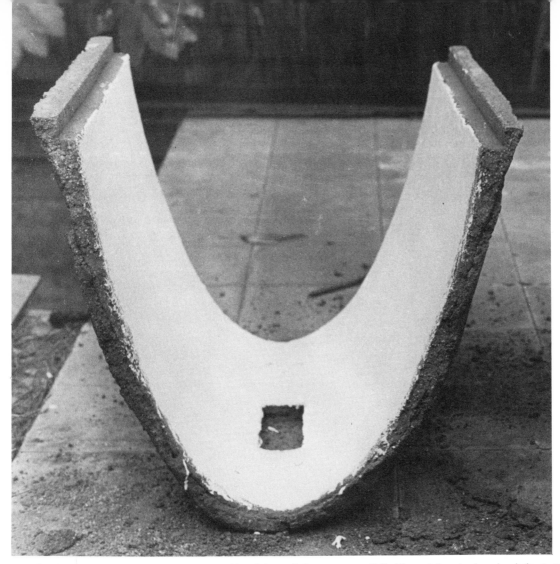

7-1. Casting a kiln may be done over the outside of the arch form or inside it.

7-2. The arch form is placed arch down, and casting mix is tamped onto the inside surface.

plastic squeegee across the surface of the mix, or rolling across it with a small wooden rolling pin.

The material should be left to rest until the binders in the mix set up and harden completely. Until the mix is totally cured, make no attempt to remove the arch form from the fresh casting, since this could weaken the casting considerably. When it is ready, the arch form, with the casting still in place, can be turned back to an upright position, and the arch form removed from the casting inside. Withdraw the nails or other fastening devices, and simply pull the masonite shell away, exposing the casting.

The casting itself now appears to be a totally enclosed form containing both the front and back walls as a continuing part of the arch itself—without door, flue, or burner ports. To make a door, simply cut one end of the casting out with a saw after first drawing an outline of the desired door shape and size directly on the outside of the cast kiln. Using a pointed keyhole saw, create an opening for the point of the saw and cut the door where marked. Make the saw cut at an inward angle so that the door will have a bevel which will stop it and not allow it to fall into the kiln when it is reinserted. The flue opening can be cut out directly on top of the cast arch form in the same fashion. If the kiln will be a downdraft system instead of an updraft one, you need not cut a flue out of the top of the arch. Burner ports can be cut out of the bottom of the casting either at the rear or on the side of the kiln.

A small cast kiln needs no burner ports whatsoever. The kiln is simply placed on a wall of bricks which already provides for burner ports. (Fig. 7–3.)

Instead of the interior casting that has been described, exterior casting of the catenary arch can be done, but such a procedure is recommended only for a kiln greater than ten cubic feet. The procedure for tamping the mix on the exterior is the same as that described for the interior of the arch form, with the one basic difference in approach simply being that the arch form is placed flat down, arch up. (Fig. 7–4.) Mark the burner ports and the flue opening of such a kiln on the arch form before you apply the mix. When you reach the marked-off area, leave it free of mix. The front door can be cast in place with a strip of plastic sheeting used along the outer edge between the front of the arch wall, as a separator, so that after the door casting has cured, it can be lifted away from the face of the arch form. No cutting is required.

Casting a kiln on the outside of the arch form is somewhat more limiting than casting it on the inside. Since the finished inside of the cast kiln should be smooth and without surface cavities, exterior casting often requires a reworking of this interior surface to fill in and smooth the surface. In addition, interior corners are not as accessible for reinforcement.

7–3. A small cast kiln need not have burner ports within it since these are provided in the brick wall underneath, as shown here.

7–4. Tamping mix on the outside of the arch form.

The Mix

The casting mix recommended is one of the recently developed lightweight ceramic-fiber casting materials. Vari-Form B is an extremely strong material after curing, very much like cement in appearance, and with a good tensile strength. It is a composition of ceramic fibers combined with a binder which gives it hydrothermal setting action during its curing period. This means that the water content in the mix develops heat during curing in the same manner as plaster does during its setting-up period. For best results, this mix must be correctly portioned with water as indicated in the preliminary data sheet sent along by the company.

In order to set properly, Vari-Form B must remain undisturbed at room temperature for a period of not less than eighteen hours after casting. An overabundance of water during the mixing procedure will contribute to a slightly weaker density of the cast material. The mix should be kept as close to the required 50-lb. density as possible.

Experience has shown that a minimum of 175 lbs. of Vari-Form B are required to cast a 2″-thick layer of this mix over the surface of the twelve-cubic-foot catenary arch form illustrated in chapter 2. Two inches of this material is equivalent to fifteen inches of refractory firebricks.

Vari-Form B is rated by the manufacturer to have a thermal working temperature of 2,400°F., but experience has proven that temperatures approaching this level tend to create surface cracks in the material which deepen with further use and, as a result, considerably weaken the entire structure. Therefore, the maximum heat used within the kiln should be kept to cone six, or not more than 2,200°F., to prevent structural deterioration.

Three things can be done to increase substantially the strength and working properties of this casting mix: application of a heavy coating of ceramic-fiber liquid cement upon the interior surface of the cured casting; embedding lath wire one inch into the center of the tamping mix during application onto the arch form; and the use of colloidal-silica liquid, instead of water, to proportion the mix for tamping. (See ch. 8 for properties of colloidal silica.) If necessary, all three of these additional things can be applied consecutively during the casting procedure to develop greater strength and reliability in the final form.

When additional insulation seems warranted, a covering of ½″-thick ceramic-fiber thermal blanket can be laid over the outside of the casting; this will help return heat to the inside chamber by preventing heat loss through the outside. The casting can also be sandwiched between two layers of thermal blanket — one on the outside and the other on the inside. You can insert a series of Nichrome wire pins through the wall of the casting to hold the internal blanket in place. The casting can easily be penetrated with a drill bit to insert the wires. If you use a high-temperature blanket inside the cast arch, the kiln is then operational at cone ten or better. (For details on anchoring a ceramic-fiber blanket to an internal surface, see ch. 4.)

Another new and relatively interesting method for casting a catenary kiln is one which uses a ceramic-fiber blanket along with Carborundum's LDS Moldable casting mix. The casting mix is a vital part of the kiln, however, in that it acts as the structural support as well as an insulating agent. The manufacturer's recommended method of construction for this experimental kiln is to place the catenary arch form in the upright, bottom-down, position for casting on its exterior surface. A half-inch-thick covering of high-temperature ceramic-fiber blanket rated at 2,600°F. is laid over the entire form, and this blanket is then coated with ceramic-fiber liquid cement and a second layer of half-inch ceramic-fiber blanket is laminated to the first. The second blanket, however, is rated at 2,300°F. After the two blankets have been put in place over the arch form, apply LDS Moldable casting material, one inch thick, over the blanket.

Carborundum's LDS Moldable is a relatively new product which has very little shrinkage. The manufacturer specifies that direct 2,000°F. exposure to this material will result in only 2 percent shrinkage after twenty-four hours of constant use. Made of ceramic fibers and binders, LDS is packaged and wet premixed, ready for application. Its density is 40 lbs. per square foot, which gives it a good tensile strength. When applying it, use gloves or a towel to protect the hands from irritation caused by the fiber particles.

Updraft and Downdraft Cast Kilns

The basic principles of the cast catenary kiln used as an updraft system are similar to those described in chapter 2, for the twelve-cubic-foot updraft kiln. The manner in which heat is circulated through the kiln chamber remains basically the same regardless of the insulating material used; the key to control lies in your recognizing that heat starting in the bottom of the kiln and moving upward must go through the kiln chamber before it finds its way out of the flue. Learning to retain the heat so that it does not get out of the kiln too quickly—this is the secret of successful updraft firing. (For more specific techniques on controlling heat in an updraft system, see ch. 4.)

As mentioned earlier, regardless of the composition of its insulating materials, the cast kiln has its burners in the lower floor region. The burner ports, therefore, are provided for in the cast body of the kiln or located in the brick wall under the footing of the cast kiln. (Fig. 7–5.) Keep in mind that the most effective heat circulation system for the updraft catenary is initiated through the side of the kiln. Here the flame thrusts itself up into the curvature of the arch and into the ware stacked below before leaving the kiln on its final ascent out the flue.

The same cast kiln can also be operated as a downdraft system, with the insulating floor arrangement somewhat altered. A cast kiln designed for a downdraft system must not have an opening in the top of its arch, although it would be possible to cut a flue out and then later replace the plug that provided the opening. A downdraft cast kiln requires burner ports on only one side of the arch form. There can be either two or three ports, depending upon the required B.t.u. for the size of the stacking chamber. The kiln floor must have a recessed chamber leading to the opposite side of the burner ports and terminating outside the exterior wall. (Fig. 7–6.) Outside of the kiln wall, where the channel terminates, place a stack. Provide for a damper slot that accommodates a damper shelf to regulate heat flow out of the kiln during firing operations. Place a bag wall inside the kiln, on the burner ports side, to baffle the flame and protect the ware from direct impingement. Across the remaining portion of the floor outside the bag wall, put in a superficial floor with open chinks. This secondary floor allows the flame to move out of the firebox—inside the confines of the bag wall—and flow up into the curvature of the arch, where it circulates through the ware before driving downward to the floor channel and outward through the stack on the outside of

the kiln. This flame flow circulation—from firebox enclosure on one side of the kiln through the floor and out the stack on the other side—is referred to as a "crossdraft" system and is very effective and very efficient in the use of fuel. (For further details regarding the principles of the downdraft system, see ch. 3.)

A minor modification of this downdraft system involves the use of a low insulating brick wall upon which the cast kiln rests. In this case, the burner ports and flue opening are built into the wall rather than into the casting. The flue opening in the insulating-brick retaining wall must have a damper system constructed as detailed in chapter 3. (See Fig. 7–6.)

7–5. Burners are inserted in the supporting course of bricks under the cast kiln.

Downdraft Adaptation for Cast Kiln

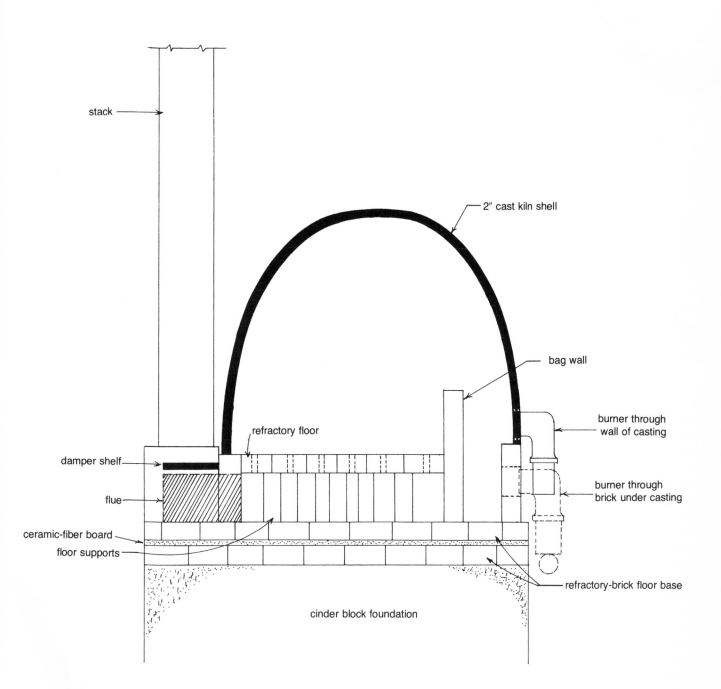

stack

2″ cast kiln shell

bag wall

burner through
wall of casting

refractory floor

damper shelf

burner through
brick under casting

flue

ceramic-fiber board

floor supports

refractory-brick floor base

cinder block foundation

Kiln Floor and Base

The cast kiln floor and foundation should have the following basic provisions: The foundation should be sufficiently high enough off of the ground level so as not to create a hardship during loading and unloading. The floor must be constructed of insulating material that will withstand the temperatures used as well as be strong enough to support the weight of posts and refractory shelves resting upon it. Construction of the foundation is simply resolved by using cement cinder blocks. You have at least two possible options in the construction. The floor can be constructed entirely of hard refractory bricks as described in ch. 2, or you can construct it from a combination of insulating bricks and compressed ceramic-fiber board. If you take the latter option, it would be both more economical in cost and labor to utilize compressed ceramic-fiber board or ceramic-fiber block. These compressed materials can easily be cut with a hand saw, leaving very little waste.

On the kiln base, first lay down a sheet of ½" compressed ceramic-fiber board, then another layer of ceramic-fiber blanket over this. The blanket should be high-temperature 2,600°F. material if the kiln is to be used in the stoneware range. Place the cast kiln upon the base insulating material. Next, put shelf posts in position and shelves upon the posts in order to allow them to seat themselves in the soft flooring. The order of this construction can be reversed by using the blanket first, then placing the compressed board on top of the blanket. Where seams need to be filled or joints caulked, you can use ceramic-fiber liquid cement.

Ceramic-fiber block can be used under the sides, back, and front of the cast kiln in order to lift the kiln up off the floor; the blocks should be 2" thick, with burner ports cut into them if it is a downdraft kiln. The block literally supplements any sort of bricks you use. Keep in mind that any ceramic-fiber materials that are a part of the cast kiln flooring must be used within the limits of their rated hot face use. This means that the face of the material exposed to the heat inside the kiln should not be heated in excess of its temperature usage. Although ceramic-fiber materials will not melt unless a temperature exceeding 3,600°F. is reached, they *will* change character somewhat, becoming brittle and shrinking a little. Take these factors into special consideration when you use ceramic-fiber materials in the kiln firebox area.

The Door

If you use a Vari-Form B casting, the door can be secured to the front of the kiln with standard metal hinges. You can counter sink the holes for the hinges directly into the cast kiln body, matching the position for the door and also for the door slab. The holes should be made slightly undersized so the screws will secure themselves tightly to the door. Use a heavy-duty wood screw to anchor the hinges—not a bolt and nut, since the nut will oxidize and crumble away if exposed inside the kiln. You can attach a latch for the door in the same manner. Another approach to securing a door on a cast kiln is to screw a metal tab at the top of the front of the arch. Put the door, which has been cut at a bevel, in place like a plug and rotate the tab down across the door to hold it in position. Figure 7–7 illustrates that standard drawer handles can be screwed onto the door.

7–7. Handles and a metal locking tab can be screwed directly into the cured casting of the kiln arch and door.

Burner System

Two types of burner systems can be designed for the cast catenary kiln. One system, designed specifically for a small kiln less than ten cubic feet in size, is operated with a squirrel-cage blower which feeds air to the fuel being driven into the kiln. The other burner design is the same system as was developed for the twelve-cubic-foot updraft kiln discussed in chapter 2 and should be used for any cast kiln larger than ten cubic feet.

Figure 7–8 shows that the squirrel-cage burner system is made up of three basic elements: the burner pipe (made from 2″-diameter elbows and extension nipples), the fuel line (made from 3/8″ copper tubing), and the blower (attached to the 2″ tee in the center of the two burner pipes). In the diagram, the distance between burner heads is not shown; this must be calculated by measuring from the centers of the burner port openings of the cast kiln. The desired distance between burners depends upon the size of the kiln and the position of the burner ports as well as whether the type of kiln is updraft or downdraft. All burner ports are shown as standard 2″ plumbing fixtures. Squirrel-cage blowers are normally available through sources supplying home oil heaters, but they are also commonly found in scrap yards. When you acquire such a blower, make sure to measure the opening for a 2″ inside fit. Otherwise it may be necessary to make an adapter fitting out of a piece of scrap sheet metal that will slip onto the end of the blower as a sleeve which can be attached to the burner-entry tee.

7–8.
Squirrel-Cage Burner Blower

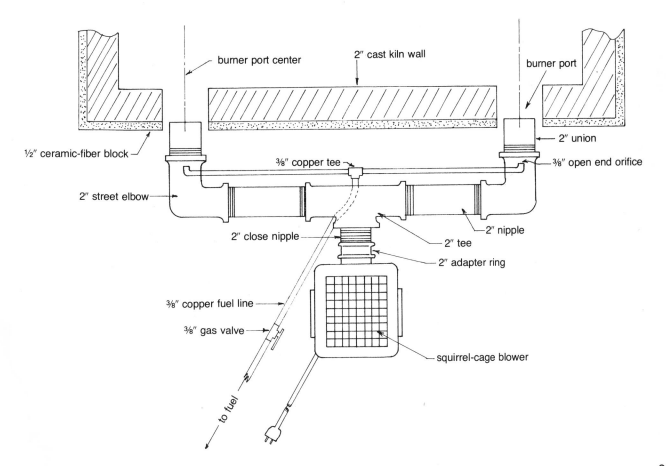

Blower Burner Operation

Notice that Figure 7–8 has no indication for an air input control cover (a regulator to control the amount of air going into the burner). Since this type of blower does not provide a forceful enough stream of air, none is necessary.

After the fuel has been ignited at the entry of the burner head, switch the blower on and allow the full flow of air to mix with the fuel. If the flame blows off of the burner heads, this means insufficient fuel input. Should this occur, first turn the fuel completely off; then, a moment later, turn the blower off. The burners can now be reignited, but with the opening of the gas valve substantially increased so that the flame from the burner heads is much more forceful than before. Again, forced air can be introduced. Now, adjust the gas input valve to trim the flame to the proper combustion consistency. This procedure allows the gas input to be pulled down slightly until a forceful yellow flame with a short blue crown just off the burner head is entering the kiln chamber. (See ch. 1 for more information about flame characteristics.)

Once the burner system is properly set and the necessary adjustments have been made, no further manipulations are needed. The flame input is now self-sustaining and will continue to build up heat inside the kiln chamber to a point of temperature maturity. Remember that this system is designed to accommodate the necessary B.t.u. for a small cast catenary kiln of less than ten cubic feet in volume, but will be most effective for a four- to six-cubic-foot kiln. You can inject more fuel into the burner system, but only at the expense of sacrificing the correct combustion of the flame, which will become smoky and less oxidizing. This, of course, is of some advantage if reduction firing conditions are desired, provided the smoke intrusion is not so excessive as to inhibit heat rise during the firing cycle.

The materials list that follows is for casting a twelve-cubic-foot catenary arch kiln using the foundation, floor, arch form, and burner system described in chapter 2. The quantities, measurements, and burner systems for cast kilns of different sizes would of necessity vary, but the types of materials remain the same.

Material List for the Twelve-Cubic-Foot Catenary Cast Kiln

Using Vari-Form B
Arch form:
See the materials list for ch. 2.

Casting mix:
175 lbs.

Ceramic-fiber liquid cement:
½ gallon

Thermal blanket:
50 sq. ft., ½″ thick, 6 lb. density, 2300°F.

Burner system:
See ch. 2, Figs. 2–13 and 2–14.

Foundation and floor:
See ch. 2.

Using LDS Moldable in Conjunction with Ceramic-Fiber
Thermal blankets

Arch form:
See the materials list for ch. 2.

Casting mix:
200 lbs.

Thermal blanket:
50 sq. ft. ½″ thick, 6 lb. density, 2600°F.
50 sq. ft. ½″ thick, 6 lb. density, 2300°F.

Ceramic-fiber liquid cement:
½ gallon

Burner system:
See ch. 2, Figs. 2–13 and 2–14.

Foundation and floor:
See ch. 2.

8. Additional Applications for Space-Age Materials

This chapter is designed to illustrate the many uses to which the new space-age materials can be put—uses which can considerably help in the repair and operation of conventional pottery kilns—and also to describe some of these materials' new commercial applications.

Ceramic-Fiber Liquid Cement

For the pottery kiln, the most versatile and widely applicable of the ceramic-fiber forms is the *cement*. Ceramic-fiber liquid cement has an off-white color and a density like heavy cream. It is made by ball-milling ceramic fibers to a powder and then adding liquid colloidal silica as a high-temperature nonorganic binder.

It is important to understand the nature of colloidal silica, the primary inorganic binder for forming rigid ceramic-fiber shapes as well as the agent for the liquid cement. Early in the thirties, laboratory research revealed that sodium could be removed from sodium silicate by means of ion exchange to produce silicic acid. At the time, this new product was used as a clarifier for the water treatment industry, but later, it was discovered that the colloidal silica also had a far stronger binding effect than sodium silicate and yet was more refractory. In fact, there are actually millions of silica particles in a single gram of water—enough to cover totally a surface area greater than 1,000 square feet. With a filler added to it, such as alumina, silica (as a powder), or other silicates such as clay, mullite, talc, mica, forsterite, or zircon, this liquid material becomes extremely resistant to any type of structural breakdown when exposed to temperatures exceeding 2,000°F. If the filler is dense, such as clay or mullite, the cement will be heavy and dense, but when a lightweight filler is added, such as powdered ceramic-fiber, the result is a liquid cement compatible with other ceramic-fiber forms like blanket, board, and all the others. The amount of filler used to give the colloidal silica sufficient body may be as much as 70 percent of the volume of liquid colloidal silica base. Since the ball-milled fiber is very absorbent, this volume can be easily accepted.

Commercially available ceramic-fiber liquid cement is not inexpensive since it is sold as a brand-name product. This implies that it is made up of a special mixture formulated by the manufacturer's research lab, and this may be true; however, the basic chemical properties remain the same regardless of brand. When purchased through foundry supply sources, colloidal silica alone is not expensive. (See suppliers list at the back of the book.) As a practical working cement for the potter in the use and repair of his kiln and kiln equipment, the effectiveness of the ceramic-fiber liquid cement is unsurpassed.

If end pieces and scraps of ceramic-fiber blanket or other ceramic-fiber forms are left over after a kiln job, you can pulverize these materials by hand and add them to the liquid colloidal silica to form a durable cement. Be sure to use protective gloves and respirator while working with dry fibers; they are so microscopic that they float in the surrounding air and can be inhaled or worked into the surface of the skin.

Sodium silicate is a water-soluble silicate glass which has a universal number of uses other than high-temperature glue. In its normal form, it can be used as an adhesive cement for gluing ceramic-fiber materials together. Almost any type of material can be glued with it: metal, refractory bricks, ceramic-fiber board, and other materials. Available almost anywhere, either as a liquid or in a dry powdered form which must then be brought into solution with a water addition, it is also relatively cheap. When applied, sodium silicate should be of a fairly thick consistency, like a lightweight honey (it is water clear). You can apply it with a brush, but the brush must be cleaned immediately with water to preserve it for future use, since sodium silicate is water resistant once it has dried. Moreover, if you allow sodium silicate to dry on the skin, it will seal pores and cause irritation. Washing thoroughly with water is the most direct way of dissolving sodium silicate.

When sodium silicate is used on surfaces that are exposed to direct heat, it will turn white and crusty and eventually peel off. Therefore it is best used as an adhesive for gluing a ceramic-fiber blanket or board in place, where its adhesive quality will not be lost even after repeated firings.

Uses for Ceramic-Fiber Liquid Cement

One of the most useful applications of ceramic-fiber liquid cement on traditionally built brick kilns is as a high-temperature glue. Many kilns built of soft insulating brick acquire repeated breaks in the bricks due to heat expansion and handling. The constant stacking and removal, by hand, of kiln doors also too often result in brick breaks. A brick can be renewed by painting ceramic-fiber liquid cement onto both exposed broken surfaces, pressing the pieces together, and placing the brick back in its normal position. After the next firing, when the cement on the broken brick seam has been exposed to above 1,200°F. heat, the seal will hold continuously. If the brick breaks again, it is highly unlikely that the break will occur at the same location. (Fig. 8–1.)

Ceramic-fiber liquid cement can also be used as a caulking material for filling in narrow cracks in internal walls of a kiln. The walls can be soft insulating or hard refractory bricks since the bonding effect is the same.

The entire inner surface of a kiln constructed with hard refractory bricks can be coated with ceramic-fiber cement to help deflect some of the heat normally absorbed by this brick. The brick's basic nature will not be changed through such an application, but, to some degree, the brick will thereafter reflect rather than radiate heat as is characteristic of dense refractory material. (In Fig. 8–2, ceramic-fiber liquid cement is being applied to the inner surface of the twelve-cubic-foot cast kiln.)

External as well as internal surfaces can be coated with ceramic-fiber liquid cement. Areas around chimney stacks requiring bonding can be cemented. (Fig. 8–3.) For the most effective bond, the cement should be exposed to 1,200°F. heat or more, because at this temperature the silicates in the cement fuse together to develop a binding strength.

You can brush the cement on the inside of burner port walls to protect the area from flame abrasiveness. Even though the cement does not expand or contract if applied across brick joints, it will move with the brick face in succeeding firings. You can apply it directly to the metal surface of burner heads to protect the heads from oxidizing and scaling off during use. Other metal surfaces that protrude into the heated area of a kiln can also be coated for protection, but remember that metal will expand from extreme heat and the coating will scale off unless it is applied very liberally.

Ceramic-fiber forms such as blanket, block, or board can also take a cement coating in order to further strengthen their surfaces. If you apply the cement to soft surfaces such as blanket or felt, the parent material should first be stiffened with a rigidizer in order to prevent spalling. The cement is abrasive to the surface of soft fibers unless the application is made with care.

8–1. A broken insulating brick has been glued together with ceramic-fiber liquid cement to hold it together for many future firings.

8–2. Ceramic-fiber liquid cement will help create reflecting heat characteristcs for a refractory surface of a hard brick kiln.

8–3. Areas around chimney stacks such as these can be bonded with ceramic-fiber liquid cement.

In short, any area in conventional brick or "space-age" kilns that requires a protective binding or filling against high temperature can receive a coating of ceramic-fiber liquid cement. It may be used to adhere insulating bricks together, fill small expansion joints, repair flue and stack areas, cover hard brick surfaces for heat alteration, as well as to hold other ceramic-fiber forms in place. Sodium silicate liquid glue can be used in a similar fashion, but, as already mentioned, it is not practical to use it where there may be direct exposure to high temperatures.

Liquid Rigidizer

Although a useful material, liquid rigidizer has limited application for space-age kilns. A waterlike liquid, it can be clear or color-tinted, depending upon the brand and manufacturer. Colored rigidizer provides a means of identifying where the material is being applied during application. When sprayed upon soft ceramic-fiber forms like a blanket, the color helps differentiate which areas have been treated.

Rigidizer is used as a surface treating agent to increase the hardness and erosion resistance of materials such as felts, blankets, and other ceramic-fiber materials. It can be applied with a brush, roller, or sprayer. After the physical water has been removed, either by evaporation or by gentle heating, a bond takes place which stiffens the surface of the material.

Nonorganic rigidizers are simply colloidal silica in water suspension, and, as mentioned previously, colloidal silica is the liquid base for ceramic-fiber cement. Therefore, colloidal silica without a filler, such as ceramic-fiber cement, can be used in those areas of the kiln where soft forms of ceramic-fiber materials need a hardened surface. Kilns made entirely of ceramic-fiber blanket, for example, need protection to safeguard the surface of the inner walls, and so, coating the material with rigidizer is advisable. Rigidizer does not serve well as a binding glue when one material surface must be adhered to another surface. Although some bonding takes place with rigidizer, it is not altogether as effective as ceramic-fiber liquid cement, which better serves the purpose of bonding ceramic-fiber materials together.

Ceramic-Fiber Blanket

Ceramic-fiber blanket is the most versatile form of all the new materials discussed in this book. It can be applied as a complete insulating lining for an entire kiln or in small bits and pieces for caulking brick expansion joints. The outside as well as inside of the kiln can be caulked with ceramic-fiber blanket, and a better heat seal is assured when the spaces between door bricks have been caulked. (Fig. 8–4.) If caulking needs to be permanent, you can paint a coating of ceramic-fiber liquid cement over the caulking; this will develop a hard surface while bits of blanket behind the cement fill the void of the expansion joint.

Small scraps or pieces of blanket can also be used to cover any type of opening where heat should be retained. With conventional brick kilns, you can use pieces of blanket to block up burner ports after a firing is completed, and thus help prevent cold air from being drawn into the kiln. Ceramic-fiber blanket can literally be used as a damper simply by laying a piece over the flue opening. (You must sometimes hold the piece down with a length of iron or a house brick or the back pressure out of the flue opening is such that it will push the blanket material off.)

Scraps of blanket can also be used as insulated protection against welding during construction. (Fig. 8–5.)

As already indicated in chapters 2 and 3, the ceramic-fiber blanket can be applied as supplementary insulation to existing kilns. This technique of using the blanket as a backup to brick structures has equal validity whether applied to fuel or electric kilns. One major electric kiln manufacturer in the United States who has been covering the outside of its round insulating brick kilns with blanket before installing the final stainless steel cover guarantees its kilns to reach cone ten temperatures consistently because of this blanket insulation.

Because of the superb insulating qualities of the blanket when it is applied to exterior kiln surfaces, the kiln can be operated in any kind of weather conditions. Several kilns that I have constructed outside, without any type of structural enclosure, in northern areas such as Vancouver, B.C., Ontario, Canada, upper New York State, and Deer Isle, Maine, function unaffected by the extreme cold-weather conditions.

Blanket can be used on the inside hot face of a kiln, provided it is pinned onto the brick face so that it does not fall or loosen during subsequent firings. You can also use it as supplemental insulation for other types of kilns, as in Figure 8–6, which shows how the blanket was used only as a lining for the lid of a large top loading tile kiln. The body of the kiln was made of conventional cast refractory material, but a 55-gallon drum was cut in half lengthwise

and connected to make a coffin lid. The drum was then lined with blanket to create a lid for the kiln which can easily be lifted by one person.

In addition to ball-milling or hand-grinding ceramic-fiber blanket scraps for use as a filler in making up liquid cement, you can also wedge pieces of the material into a clay body that is being prepared for raku or for wet firing. (Fig. 8–7.) Inclusion of ceramic-fiber materials in clay provides the body with a resistance to thermal shock, but it also cuts down the amount of plasticity in the clay, so this last factor must be taken into account.

Composed of interlocking ceramic-fibers which make the use of binders unnecessary, ceramic-fiber blanket is a pliable material very much like a bed blanket. Two of the largest manufacturers of this material have products that differ slightly as to the length of the individual fibers, and one manufacturer claims that its material is stronger because the fiber length is longer (some 10"). However, this difference is not as important as the fact that the material has an extremely low heat conductivity. Because of the manner in which the fibers are produced, the material is lightweight and very pliable, and therefore can easily be cut by hand with a pair of scissors to form the needed shapes or lengths.

Ceramic-fiber blanket is produced in a variety of densities—from three pounds per cubic foot to over twenty pounds—and each density has a different price scale since the amount of fibers vary. Over the years, experience has shown that blanket material of 6-lb. density by ½" thickness is the best compromise for the money, because this size and density provide very good thermal insulation for most kiln applications at a price that is reasonable. Needless to say, a ½" thick blanket will have a considerably better insulating quality than material that is ¼" thick. If, however, the thinner material is a heavier density, it has about the same insulating qualities as a thicker material with less density. It is only when thickness is added to density that the insulation quality is greater. As just mentioned, when you use blanket as added insulation for a brick kiln, ½" 6 lb. density will do the job quite efficiently, but if the material is used directly against high heat, you can cut by a considerable amount the exterior heat loss (cold face) through the blanket by using denser and thicker material. This does not mean that the fiber's effectiveness is altered in any other way—only that the amount of heat loss will be limited. When heat is induced in a very rapid cycle, such as in the portable raku kiln, the loss through a relatively thin blanket will be negligible, but if high heat must be kept inside a chamber over a duration of many hours, density of insulating material definitely becomes a factor for consideration.

Ceramic-fiber blanket is normally furnished in rolls in standard sizes of one-, two-, and four-foot widths by approximately twenty-four foot lengths. A few distributors are beginning to supply ceramic-fiber materials to individual craftsmen in small lots rather than the large minimum quantities which manufacturers commonly require. As craftsmen's demands for these materials increase, this practice will certainly become more common.

The material is also available as a "wet blanket," in which case it comes packed in a plastic bag to retain the saturation of the presoaked binder. After removal from the bag, the blanket can then be form fitted over irregular surfaces, cut to fit those surfaces, and then dried in place. This procedure results in a stiff blanket form contoured to the shape of the surface to which it was fitted. This kind of wet blanket is useful for the construction of the cast catenary kiln described in chapter 7.

Blanket with aluminum-foil backing, which can be ordered by special request, serves well as exterior insulation for brick kilns, protecting the kiln from weather elements. The foil also reflects back into the blanket some of the cold-face heat that is being released from within the kiln.

The versatility of ceramic-fiber blanket makes it one of the most practical of the ceramic-fiber forms for use in kiln insulation and repair. It can be used either in its manufactured form or transformed into many other forms by means of ridigizer, cutting, forming, plugging, grinding, or compressing.

8–5. Ceramic-fiber blanket scraps can be used as insulation protection during welding operations.

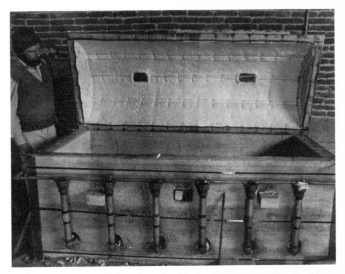
8–6. Ceramic-fiber blanket lines the lid of a large top-loading tile kiln.

8–7. Pulverized ceramic-fiber mixed into clay body will provide resistance to thermal shock during raku or wet firings.

8–4. A better heat seal is assured when door brick chinks have been caulked with pieces of ceramic-fiber blanket, as shown here.

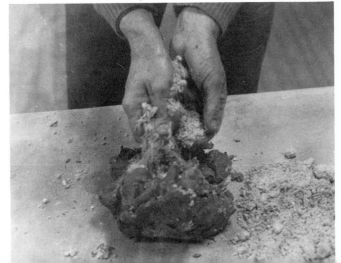

Ceramic-Fiber Compressed Board and Block

Ceramic-fiber board and block differ from each other only in that the block is thicker than the board. Block usually starts at a half inch thickness and increases to as much as two inches. Normally it has a reasonably hard crust on all exterior surfaces but is pliable internally. Ceramic-fiber board, considerably thinner than block, is not usually greater than one-quarter inch. The rigidizing material used in board has bonded the entire body of fibers, resulting in a material of consistent structure and strength throughout. The tensile strength of these materials, when rigidized, is substantial but not great. After exposure to a heat of 2,300 to 2,600°F., their tensile strength decreases slightly. Remember, it is not the tensile strength of the material that makes it so unique, but rather the low heat conductivity and lightweight insulation qualities.

Several uses for ceramic-fiber board and block have been described in previous chapters. A few of the uses are: as an insulating heat barrier on the floor of a kiln, under the first course of refractory bricks; as walls under a cast kiln; as a stable floor on the base of a drum kiln; as complete kiln doors; and as heat-retaining shields butted against the outside of a stack brick door.

Ceramic-Fiber Casting Mixes

Ceramic-fiber casting mixes are practical materials if they are prepared properly. As supplementary insulating material on conventional brick kilns, casting mix can be applied in much the same manner as blanket scrap or bulk fibers. Whereas dry blanket scrap must be coated with a ridigizer or cement to give it hardness, the casting mix already has the hardener within it at the time of application; it is simply a matter of allowing the mix to cure before exposing it to excessive heat.

Casting mixes are made up of ceramic fibers combined with inorganic hydraulic binders. This means that when the dry mix is combined with water, a hydraulic action occurs similar to the setting of plaster or concrete. After several hours, the mix first heats up while the setting action takes place, then cools off and turns into a hard, strong material. During the mixing operation, keep as close as possible to the manufacturer's suggested water proportions, since an overabundance of water will inhibit the hydraulic action and make the casting weak—a problem that will not necessarily be evident until the casting is exposed to its first high-temperature fire. After the first

firing, the casting will then develop hairline cracks which become more pronounced after each firing. The cracks must be filled in with ceramic-fiber liquid cement but if the damage is too extensive, patching becomes fruitless. Another consideration is the physical mixing of the casting material: Extensive mixing by hand or machine may shorten the ceramic fibers and this can result in a weakening of the casting after curing. Overmixing breaks down the fibers by not allowing them to interlock as efficiently during the curing period.

Mixing factors become more of a problem when the casting material is used for casting an entire kiln—especially one larger than six cubic feet. When the casting material is used in a small restricted area for caulking expansion joints between bricks or as a filler around flue stacks or around burner ports, the mixing preparation is not so crucial. (Fig. 8–8.)

Casting mixes usually are packaged in 50-lb. lots and manufacturers charge by the pound. When handled dry, these materials float excessive particles in the surrounding air, so it is advisable to wear a mask or respirator for protection against breathing the fibers. Although once wetted, the material is no longer a problem, hands should still be protected with rubber gloves to prevent short fibers from penetrating the skin, which can be quite irritating. In its prepared form, the mix will conform to almost any surface, and a one- to two-inch thickness of the mix will adhere to vertical surfaces and remain in position during the curing period. If no surface bond is desired, put a separator, such as thin plastic sheeting, between the mix and the surface upon which it is applied.

8–8. Ceramic-fiber casting mix is being used for caulking expansion joints between bricks.

Other Ceramic-Fiber Forms

Paper, stripping, spray mixes, and vacuum-formed shapes are some ceramic-fiber forms so specialized that their application to the potter's kiln is somewhat limited compared to the ceramic-fiber materials already mentioned.

All ceramic-fiber forms have the same basic thermal characteristics in terms of high-heat tolerance (above 2,000°F.), and are extremely lightweight because of the way in which the fibers are made.

Ceramic-fiber paper can be used in much the same manner as the blanket, except that paper is very thin and does not have the tensile strength of the blanket, so that its usefulness is limited. It becomes impractical to purchase only stripping unless you are using a large quantity to fill expansion joints on a big production kiln. If needed, stripping can easily be cut out of blanket rolls. Spray mixes require specialized spray equipment that can handle coarse material. Essentially, ceramic-fiber liquid cement does on a small scale what spray mixes do on a large scale.

Vacuum-formed shapes require very sophisticated equipment which is normally out of the individual potter's range. For manufacturers, however, vacuum-formed ceramic-fiber shapes are quite valid, since they totally eliminate the need for assembling or shaping, and thus manual labor is minimal. Already ahead of their time, a few companies in the United States are manufacturing kilns and furnaces on a production-line basis by means of the vacuum-form process. Lindberg Industries in Watertown, Wisconsin, for example, has developed a method called Moldatherm, in which a preformed and annealed Kanthal heating element is placed on a male vacuum molding fixture which is immersed in a proprietary slurry of ceramic fibers. The "green" form of ceramic-fiber slurry is deposited on the assembly, encasing the heating element within the insulating body. As one watches the assembly being lowered into the ceramic-fiber slurry, then reappearing as a completely finished form that includes the embedded electrical resistance coil, one realizes that this is a preview of the manufactured kilns of the future. Figure 8–9 shows one of Lindberg's Moldatherm furnaces—a one-unit form containing embedded heating elements which will bring the heat chamber up to 2,200°F. in twelve minutes. It saves 95 percent of the electrical power required to bring a conventional brick furnace to the same temperature level.

8–9. Lindberg's Moldatherm furnace is made by vacuum-forming ceramic fibers with imbedded electrical heating elements.

In January, 1974, I was issued a patent for a portable kiln utilizing the ceramic-fiber vacuum-formed system—a kiln that is totally homogeneous in structure. Designed to provide an efficient, relatively lightweight, and mechanically strong device, it can easily be disassembled and moved without strain or fear of mechanical damage and can also be easily reassembled and ready for use in a relatively short period of time. Although Figure 8–10 shows a very specific configuration, the patent was for a kiln that can be heated electrically or converted for firing with a natural fuel.

Conversion is accomplished simply by changing the lid to one that has a flue opening. The bottom member is changed in the same fashion, with a hole for the mounting of a burner being placed in position to direct heat up into the kiln chamber. Although the diagram illustrates a cylinder-shaped kiln, the basis of the patent is broad enough to encompass any other form.

8–10.

Colson Vacuum-Formed Kiln, U.S. Patent No. 3,786,162.

Magna 904 Heat Ban

One of the most interesting recent developments in high-temperature insulation is a product referred to by the manufacturer as Magna 904 Heat Ban. This jelly-like compound will absorb and dissipate heat in the high-temperature range of 2,000°F. and higher and could theoretically be used as a skin covering that would protect the hands when they enter a heated kiln chamber. When heat comes in contact with Magna 904, it is absorbed into the compound in the way that a sponge soaks up water. Instead of becoming saturated with heat, the gel channels the heat through itself and releases it to the atmosphere like no other known material, according to the manufacturer. It does not become liquid or runny when subjected to heat; it retains the same consistency irrespective of extreme temperature changes.

Magna 904 has no unpleasant odor, does not give off irritating fumes when in use, and is reputed to be completely harmless to human skin. Even if taken orally, it is harmless. After using it, you can wipe it off with a dry cloth and clean further with flushing water. It has an indefinite shelf life as long as it is in a nonhardened state and remains a jelly compound.

The manufacturer claims that Magna 904 is nontoxic and absolutely safe to use on any material or finish. You can therefore put it on pottery surfaces, fire the pottery, and find the surface covered with Heat Ban relatively unaffected. It is most effective, however, when you use it as an external heat protection that absorbs and disperses the heat into the atmosphere.

9. Troubleshooting

Some suggestions for dealing with specific malfunctions of a particular kiln have already been made in individual chapters of this book, but what follows is a general description of problems that commonly occur during kiln firing cycles.

Any new or unfamiliar kiln is an unknown kiln, and one general rule that bears repeating is that every fuel-fired kiln has its own peculiar mannerisms. With a new kiln, these mannerisms are virtually unknown—in spite of the fact that there might be an instruction booklet describing step by step how it should be fired. How to fire the kiln is one thing, but how it will perform, at least initially, is quite another. Regardless of the make, design, or construction of the kiln, it is going to take you six to ten firings to learn its mannerisms; the larger number of firings is more apt to be the case.

Even a kiln already fired a great number of times is unknown to a potter who has not operated it. The kiln performs best for the potter who has worked with it, learned its functions, and understands its mannerisms. Even then, the kiln will undergo subtle changes in its firing characteristics over a period of years. The potter who stays with his kiln during this time will recognize and understand these alterations. He knows that the kiln goes through changes with use—that bricks shift, expansion joints open, shelves crystallize, posts fracture, and stacking space shifts—each change releasing a little more heat than before. In the sense that it is always changing the kiln is very human.

Kilns built partially or entirely with ceramic fibers are a little less known than conventional kilns because the new materials create different heat effects than with kilns made from refractory or insulating bricks. Understanding how these new materials function is an asset when you are trying to discover the characteristics of such a kiln. The more ceramic-fiber materials used in a particular kiln, the more important it becomes to understand how the materials function, since this knowledge tells you what to look for when trouble begins.

Heat Problems

The primary function of any kiln is to produce controlled energy or heat. How heat enters the kiln, moves within the kiln, affects the pottery within, and how it leaves the kiln is what determines success and failure in firing. Heat initiation always begins at the burner nozzle. To control the heat, you should understand the extensive subject of burners, fuel combustion, and flame distribution which is discussed in chapter 1. Assuming that flame and combustion are properly set for kiln heating, the next likely heat problem within the kiln would be the unevenness in the overall heat of the kiln after a given temperature has been reached. The solution to this problem involves heat distribution and heat circulation.

As pointed out in previous chapters, distribution of heat inside the kiln relates to two factors: baffling and stacking.

In a downdraft kiln, the heat generated in the firebox may be forced either too high or too low into the kiln chamber to give even heat. The width of the firebox may be too restricted, thus preventing the flame from moving out and establishing a circuit of its own in the chamber. The firebox baffle wall may also contribute to flame direction and cause a hot top or a hot bottom within the kiln. (See ch. 1.)

Heat distribution in an updraft kiln is very different. The concept of the updraft kiln provides for a continuing stack where heat is emitted at one end, carried upward in a draft, and dissipated out the other end. Updraft kilns are not as well accepted as downdraft kilns because one end is always hotter than the other. This unevenness in heat frequently results in a difference in temperature of one cone or more from top to bottom. Moving heat through an updraft system is definitely more difficult, primarily because it takes considerable manipulation of the kiln baffling system to learn how to hold and distribute the heat within the chamber. The objective is to obstruct the heat from moving too rapidly up through the kiln chamber toward the flue exit, and this is done by placing shelves within the kiln in such a manner as to force heat to move back on itself for a period of time before it escapes out the flue. (See ch. 4 and Fig. 4–23.) It may take several firings before you arrive at the shelving position that will best result in even heat saturation and eliminate inconsistencies. Interestingly enough, almost all commercially manufactured pottery kilns are updraft systems, and although the manufacturer usually provides a set of specific instructions for firing their kilns, these instructions usually result in inconsistent heat saturation, with a difference in temperature of up to two cones.

The way pottery is stacked influences the circulation of heat in a kiln. Operators of commercial potteries, which produce repeated clay forms, learn to organize kiln stacking so as to provide the most efficient heat saturation with every firing. The potter who produces individual pieces, each unique unto itself, is faced with a different stacking situation every time he loads the kiln. It is often necessary for him to change the basic stacking arrangement with every firing, in order to accommodate different types and sizes of pieces. Generally, however, a pattern can be found which will best establish a direction for even heat circulation. Small pieces of pottery that are similar in height should be placed in the same area of the kiln each time, and larger pieces are also put in the same location at every stacking. This produces relative consistency, allowing you to watch each firing and recognize the effect of saturation as heat circulates during the firing cycle. At the next stacking, you can make minor adjustments that will

further help the circulation of heat until eventually the inconsistencies will be narrowed to almost nothing and you will be able to take even heat for granted.

Incorrect heat circulation can cause dangerous alterations, such as the blowing out of a wall or door, or even the complete collapse of a kiln. This happens when the basic mechanical design of a downdraft kiln has been changed. All downdraft kilns must have a means of allowing heat from the firebox to pass under the stack area—where pottery is placed—to the flue opening. Normally you leave this area vacant by placing a false floor above it, structuring the false floor in such a manner as to allow flame, after it has circulated through the ware, to pass through this floor and out the flue below. Should this false floor under the pottery stack area ever be removed and pottery stacked in its place, heat would be inhibited from moving freely out of the flue opening on the opposite side. Figure 9–1 shows how an interior or false floor set at a level above the flue opening allows flame to be pulled downward instead of across, as would be the case if no raised floor existed. This system helps to develop *even* instead of *uneven* circulation, and the possibility of a fuel "pile-up" is avoided.

Figure 9–2 shows how placing pots directly on the floor creates a secondary baffle effect in front of the flue, in addition to the bag wall which is already restricting the flame. This extra baffle created by the density of the pottery stacking cuts draft to a minimum. The seriousness of this condition will vary with the density of stacking in front of the flue opening.

In a situation like the one depicted in Figure 9–2, a pile-up of raw gas that is improperly combusted or not combusted at all results. Some combustion may be evident in the form of a flame. In any case, excessive uncombusted gas continues to pour into the floor cavity until the fuel becomes so rich that ignition suddenly takes place in the form of an explosion. At first it may appear that the burners faulted, causing the catastrophe, when actually the explosion occurred because the flue opening was partially plugged by pottery obstructing the natural draft for entering flame.

Flame circulation resulting in fuel pile-up does not occur as readily with updraft kilns, where only obvious and deliberate blockage of the flue opening would create a similar condition. Since updraft kiln flues are on top of the kiln, far from the location of heat input, they are rather difficult to obstruct. Blockage of this area would immediately create incorrect combustion, which would be recognized as such, and it is unlikely that an explosion would occur in the short span of time it would take to notice the problem.

The dangerous conditions described here are more apt to occur when you use fuels that are heavier than air. Natural gas is the only widely-used fuel which is lighter than air. Liquid gases, such as propane and butane, are heavier than air and can spread around a kiln floor totally uncombusted for several seconds, or sometimes minutes, before igniting. This can happen even with a flame at the burner tip. The flame may be extremely rich, pushing out more gas than is actually ignited. Sometimes this occurs in a "topping-off" condition in which gas pressure creates a flame only at its extended tip, while, at the source, raw gas is falling off onto the floor of the kiln or burner port. It is extremely important, therefore, that you always adjust burners for their correct air/fuel ratio in order to develop correct combustion.

Gas explosions can also occur when a series of burners are hooked up on a single manifold without individual valves. If one or more of the burners are not ignited, while the remainder are, a condition is created which places raw uncombusted fuel into a portion of the kiln chamber that is devoid of flame. Then it is only a matter of time before the uncombusted gas spreads out over a large enough area and reaches a live flame, whereupon the pile-up of uncombusted gas ignites, causing a forceful explosion. In a small kiln an explosion can result in blowing out a door or possibly shifting the shelves and pottery, but in a large production kiln, it is dangerous indeed. A strong wind can blow a burner out during the low preheating cycle. However, never take it for granted that only one burner is out on a series sharing the same manifold. An operator of a large production brick kiln once observed a single burner out and did not inspect the other burners to see if they were ignited. He lit the one burner and immediately 40,000 bricks came crashing down around him. Fortunately, he was not injured—only dazed.

Heat Stalemating

Stalemating is a firing condition that occurs when heat within the kiln reaches a given level of temperature below what is desired and will go no further, neither increasing nor falling. Many variables can contribute to heat stalemating during a firing cycle, and although it is not as common a problem as uneven heat saturation, it does occur occasionally. It is more apt to happen with first firings than after

9–1.

Correct Draft and Flame Passage

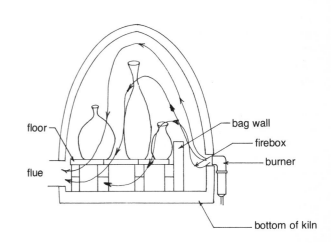

9–2.

Incorrect Draft and Flame Passage

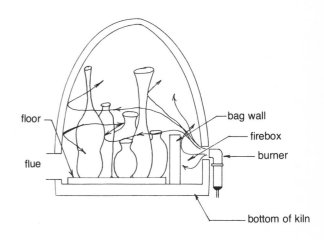

109

you have gained some experience with your kiln.

When all conditions for reaching temperature are correct, it is quite frustrating to have a stalemate heat condition develop. The normal reaction is simply to wait, hoping that more time will afford an opportunity for the condition to resolve itself. After several hours of waiting and hoping, with conditions remaining constant, doubts begin to arise. Is the draft sufficient? Is the stack high enough? Is the kiln designed properly?

The first place to look for trouble is in the fuel input system. Natural or liquid gas kilns must have sufficient volume and proper pressure in order to supply the burners with enough B.t.u. to create an increasing heat cycle in the kiln chamber. At the time the gas line installation was made, the right pressure may have been furnished, but the volume delivered under that pressure could be insufficient. Volume is controlled by two factors: the size of the pipe carrying the gas to the burners, and the size or position of the diaphragm in the regulator at the tank or meter. To use an analogy, when you water a field of grass with a garden hose containing very high pressure, the field will get watered, eventually; however, it will take a considerable amount of time. The same field, watered with a fire hose three inches in diameter and containing the same pressure as the garden hose, would cover the area in a fraction of the time. The difference is not in the pressure, but in the volume being delivered.

Natural gas should read not less than eight inches "water column pressure"—the standard term for reading natural gas pressure—and liquid petroleum gas should measure not less than eleven pounds of pressure. These suggested measurements are slightly higher than those required for household appliances and also refer to the pressure at the kiln, not the meter or tank. Volume is determined by a regulator for LPG at the tank (a high-pressure regulator should be installed); it will be sufficient when the pressure measures correctly with all burners wide open. The same applies to natural gas. While you measure pressure with all burners wide open, keep the kiln open also and make certain no flame from matches, cigarettes, or other matter is nearby. There cannot be enough emphasis put on checking gas pressure in this manner! It will be evident that correct pressure is needed during the kiln firing, when all of the burners are open, not when they are off.

I recall a particular stalemated heat condition on a hundred-cubic-foot kiln many years ago: After sitting with the kiln for thirty-six continuous hours, it was determined that pressure in the line was insufficient. The kiln was shut down. The twenty burners, which were under the internal structure of the floor and on a common manifold, were torn out of the kiln and the entire system was then reassembled outside. All but one burner was plugged up and the pressure on that one was checked. Although pressure read correctly with the system shut off, it was discovered that as soon as one burner was opened, the pressure dropped amazingly. When the remaining nineteen burners were opened and pressure checked once again, the reading was nil. The pressure was then brought up to the correct minimum amount by changing the diaphragm regulator to a much larger-sized one. The burner system was reinstalled, and from then on, no stalemate heat condition ever recurred.

Fuel pressure loss can also happen abruptly during a firing cycle. Flame going into the kiln can appear to diminish without cause. Even after you turn the gas valve up a little, a few minutes later the flame diminishes again. Finally, you open the valve completely, only to have the burners simply extinguish themselves during the very middle of a firing cycle! The cause of this mysterious turn of events is lack of pressure. This condition almost never develops with a natural gas kiln since fuel is supplied from a high-pressure main line. However, LPG can freeze in the fuel tank during a firing if the gas content drops below 30 percent of capacity—even when capacity is as high as 60 percent. High elevation can contribute to tank freezing, as was observed during the firing of a large tile kiln in Mexico at an elevation of over 7,000 feet. If you fire at night, particularly during winter months, cold outside air can also contribute to tank freezing. In Mexico, LPG is not always pure (it is often mixed with butane), and can vary from tank load to tank load. This should be taken into account.

There are several ways to resolve the problem of freezing: First, always try to "top off" the fuel tank before you start a firing. Capacity should be 80 percent or better. Second, schedule the firing during daylight hours to prevent extremely cold air from surrounding the tank at night. And third, have the fuel tank where sunlight strikes it during operation. If a large kiln is subjected to the fuel tank problems described here, you can connect two fuel tanks together on the same line. Then if one tank begins to freeze up, bring the second one into use and shut the first one off. Switching can continue as long as required.

Heat Recognition

If you recognize the signs, you can resolve most heat-related problems before they occur. You will not only be avoiding impending problems but also improving kiln operation by understanding the way heat builds up during the firing cycle.

Several pointers, in sequence, will help to recognize heat effects during the firing cycle:

1. During initial burner ignition, heat can only be identified as a form of pressure. If all peephole plugs are closed and the damper nearly closed down, heat will build up a back pressure. If you open a peephole and place a hand in front of the opening, you can easily feel the heat.

2. During early preheat stages of firing—the essential stage of drying moisture from the pottery—the kiln chamber's visible color will appear to be black. If the flame is strong enough to light up the chamber, heat input coming from inside the kiln is too strong and trouble can be expected. During the "black" firing stage of firing, heat buildup is identified by increased back pressure out of the peepholes. Another way to tell at this stage is by the slight discoloration of the clay body when you view it through the peephole area. You can assume, with some accuracy, that the temperature during this period is at least 400°F., similar to that of a kitchen oven at high-bake setting.

3. The most crucial heat period comes next. Pottery goes through one of the most important transformations of its entire heating cycle between temperatures 400 to 900°F.; this is when the so-called chemical water is driven out of the pottery. If heat is increased too rapidly, moisture turns to steam which cannot escape quickly enough from the clay body structure, and the result is a bursting of the pottery wall and usually destruction of the entire piece. Therefore, heat should build up steadily and gradually. The atmosphere of the kiln must give room for dispersion of released moisture. Color of the kiln during this period (500 to 700°F.), remains relatively dark.

4. The first visible color—faint red—appears in the kiln chamber at 900°F. With the beginning of color, the danger point is past, and the likelihood of pots exploding has virtually disappeared. As heat continues to increase, color increases proportionately. After a bright red color has developed, it is only a short time before an orange hue appears. Orange is a clear indication that heat is increasing in temperature. Assuming cone 06 to be the lowest cone, the first pyrometric cone is now about to bend over.

5. The first cone falling is proof that temperature is continuing to rise and conditions in the kiln are ready for damper adjustment in order to initiate reduction. (See ch. 1 for further information on reduction firing techniques.)

6. With reduction well along and heat continuing to rise in temperature, you may have some difficulty identifying temperature in terms of color. The chamber now appears to be a light yellow. As color becomes lighter, each succeeding cone bends and gives you a guide as to the progress of conditions in the kiln. If reduction is taking place, the atmosphere of the kiln at this point will appear hazy or foggy, but this should not distort the reading of heat color, since color remains true regardless of kiln atmosphere.

7. When final temperature is reached and the last cone has fallen, heat color will appear brilliant yellow-white at stoneware temperatures. You can close the kiln down and lower the fuel input slightly to create a deliberate stalemate condition, which is referred to as "soaking." You should develop this heat-soaking condition after the glazes are melted and temperature has been reached because it allows glazes to flow even if they had only begun to melt when temperature was reached. But soaking should not be confused with stalemating. It is a purposeful means of holding heat within the kiln at a given temperature after attaining peak temperature whereas stalemating is heat which will not continue to rise to peak temperature.

Degrees F.		Degrees C.		Firing Point
chromium	3000			refractories
	2900	1600	cone 30	
pure iron	2800			
	2700	1500	Cone 20	
nickel steel	2600			high-fired porcelain
	2500	1400		
monel metal		white	cone 15	
	2400	1300		common porcelain
manganese	2300	(3)	cone 10	
	2200	1200	(2)	C 5	studio stoneware cone 5
	2100		lt. yellow		ease-off reduction
copper	2000	1100		C02	nepheline syenite china
gold	1900		lemon	C05	
		1000			begin reduction for body
silver	1800	(1)			talc-body earthenware
	1700		orange	C08	
	1600	900	(4) salmon		
	1500	800	bright red		C010 low-fire glazes
	1400		cherry	C015	vitreous metal enamels
aluminum	1300	700	med. cherry	C018	overglaze decoration
magnesium	1200		dark cherry		
	1100	600		C020	lowest-fire glass enamels
	1000			C022	
	900	500	faint red		
zinc	800	400			dangerous period in kiln cycle, during which period
lead	700				cracking is more liable to occur, both in firing
	600	300			up and cooling down.
	500				
	400	200			
	300				
	200	100			
	100	0			
	0				

REDUCTION:
1. For clay body, reduce early C06
2. For glaze, reduce C5 upward
3. For glaze and body, start C06
and continue through firing cycle
4. *Sudden reduction saturation:*
Close all dampers before cutting fuel off.

TEMPERATURE CHART

**Melting Points of
Common Materials**

Fig. 9-3.   °F.   °C.

The temperature chart in Figure 9–3 is a practical guide to firing a kiln without a pyrometer, by means of identifying heat color. When firing, it is helpful to follow the color guides on this chart until you recognize specific heat ranges. The seven points in the preceding list will help you understand each stage that a high-temperature kiln goes through. If these steps and the chart are used together as you observe a number of kiln firings, you will be able to identify almost immediately any inconsistencies that occur during the firing cycle.

Mechanical pyrometers which are installed in a kiln heat chamber and have a Fahrenheit-degree scale are never consistently accurate, particularly in reduction firings, when a pyrometric needle becomes coated with carbon and insulates the heat-sensitizing point of the pyrometer. Pyrometric cones are by far the most accurate way to measure heat. They are placed in the center of the heat chamber and are made of clay materials, as is the pottery, and this contributes to their accuracy. However, if reduction has caused them to become heavily covered with carbon, or if they are placed near a burner port and receive "flashing," they will not indicate heat correctly.

Flashing and Hot Spots

This is a good place to discuss "flashing," the term which refers to the direct impingement of a flame upon the ware or other components within the kiln chamber. Flashing can be either detrimental or pleasing, depending on the object being flashed. Often a piece of pottery retrieved from the finished firing has a distinctive coloration mark, which has usually been caused by flame licking, or "flashing." This effect is sometimes a mark of distinction and beauty and greatly enhances the piece of pottery. The Japanese consider the mark of flashing a blessing of the flame which has distinguished the particular piece. Primitive Indian and Mexican pottery often has flashing marks which result from the effect of open-air bonfire kilns.

Normally, however, flashing is a detriment to pottery—and often a detriment to the kiln as well. A flame lick during the crucial water-vaporation stage can blow a pot to pieces. The side of the pot being struck by flame will heat up out of proportion to the rest of the piece; water will expand into steam and, before it can escape, an explosion will occur. To prevent this, the pot must be protected by placing it away from flame impingement. It can also be protected from impingement by baffling: Sections of shelves or refractory bricks are placed around the pot to safeguard it. When complete protection is needed, put pottery into a refractory container (referred to as a "sagger") in the kiln. Some old types of traditional fuel kilns were specifically designed to direct flame from the burners up through refractory tubes inside the kiln to prevent flame from entering the heat chamber. Since all flame was thus baffled away from the heat chamber, these were called "baffle kilns."

In addition to the direct effect it has on the pottery, extensive flashing can create hot spots in the heat chamber, resulting in uneven heat saturation and inconsistent firing cycles. Flashings of this kind are sometimes due to damaged or incorrect orifice openings. The same effect can result from a kiln fired with only one large burner—a burner which is putting out an enormous amount of B.t.u. and an exceptionally large flame. Many kilns operate on just such a system, but they normally have sufficient baffling to prevent long-reaching flame from entering the heat chamber.

Flashing and hot spots can also be attributed to the type of fuel used. Natural and LPG gas remains in a state of combustion at the time of ignition at the burner orifice, but heavier fuels, such as kerosene, No. 2 fuel oil, diesel oil, and others, depend upon ignition from spontaneous combustion. This means that instead of a self-sustaining ignition, as with gas or LPG, they require an external source for combustion. When a liquid fuel is released, it must be brought to combustion temperature before ignition takes place. If the liquid is transformed into a vapor, ignition occurs quite readily and the resulting combustion is forceful. During the vaporization process, however, some heavy fuels thrust particles of liquid into the kiln firebox faster than ignition can take place at the burner port, with the result that these liquid particles explode upon entry in the firebox. If this condition persists with considerable velocity, there will be a great deal of flashing. If the firebox retaining wall (bag wall) is close to the burner port entry, the flashing will be forced back out the burner ports to create what is commonly called a "flashback." This can be a dangerous condition for the kiln operator during fuel adjustments at the burner ports, so care must be taken.

All the problem areas brought to the reader's attention in this chapter pertain to any type of fuel kiln, whatever its design or construction. Whether your kiln is lined with brick or with ceramic fibers, the pottery is the primary object of any firing. To a great degree, the success of that firing depends on your understanding of the matters discussed here: heat, its source, its direction and movement, and its ultimate effects.

10. Safety Regulations and Pollution-Control Fuel Systems

Safety regulations relating to kiln installation, gas hookups, property placement, and ventilation, vary according to zoning. (Usually the regulations in ordinance books covering kilns are listed under "furnaces.") A restricted residential zone will certainly have many more limitations against the installation of a pottery kiln than a heavy industrialized zone, where such equipment is taken for granted. However, I have constructed pottery kilns in highly restricted residential areas—Miami Beach and Vancouver—as well as in virtually unzoned districts in Mexico and Australia, where practically anything goes. No matter what the location is, you should take into account a number of common-sense rules before you construct a kiln of any considerable size.

A personal experience with zoning regulations may be a good introduction to this discussion. Several years ago, construction on a large eighty-cubic-foot roll-in kiln was started in a restricted zoning area. A local complaint was made, and in no time a city building inspector came around. He glanced at the completed catenary arch which rose above him and asked to see the building permit for the structure. I replied that it was not a structure, but rather a piece of equipment for pottery making, and that furthermore this equipment was portable. (It had been a hundred-cubic-foot kiln the week before at another location and had been dismantled for reconstruction at its present site.) This kiln had no bonding mortar in its brick to make it in any way permanent. Still, the building inspector would not accept the kiln as a piece of equipment and repeated that it was an enclosed structure requiring a building permit. I asked the inspector to return the next day so that I could present him with proof that the kiln was indeed a piece of equipment. In the interim, ten large burners were installed on the kiln, and three large pots, measuring 60″ high, were put into the firing chamber. Upon his return, I asked the inspector to step into the "structure," along with the floor vases, while the kiln was turned on in order to bring it up to cone ten temperature well over 2300°F. From that day on, there was never any more question as to whether the kiln was a structure or a piece of equipment.

I do not mean to imply with this story that a license would be given to any person who uses such an approach in order to come within zoning regulations. In my case, the property on which the kiln was built was already zoned to conduct business as an art school, and the issue was a matter of defining whether the kiln was necessary to the operation.

In areas of dense to medium population, the most sensible approach for avoiding regulation problems is first to request that the local fire chief inspect the proposed kiln site. This step serves two protective purposes: since the chief knows the local fire ordinances, he is usually willing to advise where the best location for the kiln will be; also, since the chief is now aware of the kiln and its location in the area, if a neighbor sights a flame coming out of a tall stack or a flue opening in the evening dusk and calls the local fire department, it is unlikely that roaring fire engines and screeching wailing sirens will head for the kiln firing. Tell the fire chief the nature of the kiln and what temperatures are expected. If it is an updraft kiln which will show flame out of the flue opening, explain why this is a natural occurrence with the kiln. Naturally, explain these kiln characteristics to the neighbors too, but do so *after* construction is finished and the kiln is ready to fire, not before!

You should be aware of the following general rules when you build a kiln:

1. Do not install a kiln near inflamable vapors or explosive mixtures.

2. Loss of pressure between the gas regulator and the kiln should not exceed 0.5 inches of water-column pressure.

3. No pipeline should provide more than a maximum pressure of 15 cubic feet per hour.

4. No device other than a filter screen is to be placed inside the pipeline in order not to obstruct the flow of gas.

5. LPG is heavier than air and adequate ventilation must be provided.

  a. Butane is a liquid at below 31°F.

  b. Propane becomes a liquid when below 44°F.

6. Kilns located inside buildings or confined areas must have a source of ventilation from the outside; normally a draft-hood device is required. A rule of thumb is that 1 square inch of opening per 5,000 B.t.u. per hour of total input should be provided.

7. Electric ignition systems should ignite only at the pilot.

8. When a flame has an automatic safeguard shutoff, the response time required to shut off the gas line should not exceed 20 seconds.

9. Gas must be odorized. This is achieved by the use of 1 pound of ethyl mercaptan, 1 pound of thiophene, or 1.4 pounds of amyl mercaptan per 8,300 gallons of compressed gas.

10. Approved flexible hose can be used on devices which are necessarily portable.

This list by no means covers all regulations for all facets of fuel installation, but simply indicates several of the common considerations from the ordinance point of view in many localities. Normally, the fuel service man installing a line, meter, regulator, or fuel tank already knows many of the local regulations and can be very helpful in making suggestions. He could tell you, for example, that the installation of an above-ground LPG tank requires a certain minimum distance from the kiln site; however, the same tank may have to be placed a very different distance if buried below ground. (In addition, it is advisable to

situate an LPG tank where it will receive sunlight most of the day to help prevent freezing of the tank during operation, as discussed in ch. 9.)

Along with regulations, ordinances, and zoning limitations, here are common sense rules about things to avoid, in addition to the obvious rules already mentioned in chapter 9:

1. Do not place face and eyes close to a peephole while a kiln is at high temperature and under back pressure for reduction. Your eyebrows can disappear very quickly, not to mention the damage that could befall the eyes.

2. Do not light a forced air burner with the blower off. Light it while the blower is in operation, with the air intake shutter closed down. If the fuel does not ignite, the line can be shut off and the air intake shutter opened to clear out uncombusted fuel immediately.

3. Do not construct large kilns near wooden walls or buildings. Always allow plenty of room for air circulation around a kiln, its stack, and the burner system if such a system is externally mounted.

4. Do not take for granted that the internal areas of burners will remain clean. When reduction firing takes place, burners often become restricted because of carbonization. The burners must be cleaned out from time to time, and the same goes for burner orifices.

5. Do not abuse ceramic-fiber materials during installation or use. The fibers will last for years if you handle them with care.

6. Do not assume that ceramic fibers will hold heat like bricks during the cooling cycle. It may be necessary to "down-fire" an all-ceramic-fiber insulated kiln. (See ch. 4.)

7. Do not put a hot portable raku kiln away in the back of a car or closet. First check that the burner and other parts have cooled.

8. Do not place excessive weight upon ceramic-fiber board being used as damper shelves, since this material has low tensile strength and may break. If handled carefully, however, ceramic-fiber board can be used indefinitely as a damper shelf or door covering.

9. Do not start a firing with wet ceramic-fiber liquid cement or wet casting mix. The binders in the mix must be slowly dried before they are exposed to high temperature; otherwise, the material may boil and scale off.

10. Do not make ceramic-fiber repairs (filling, caulking, cementing, for example) with noncompatible materials such as asbestos fibers, brick mortar mix, and kiln wash. Incompatible materials will usually spall off and not work with ceramic-fiber material because their thermal properties are different in terms of heat tolerance.

11. Do not rush when applying ceramic-fiber materials. None of these materials set fast. Reserve plenty of time to make applications carefully and precisely.

Pollution Control and Fuel Systems

Although abundant information is currently available on the composition and nature of organic fuels, little has been brought to light regarding the pollution-causing effects of most conventional fuels during the kiln reduction-firing cycle. As discussed in chapter 1, organic fuels are necessary for creating a reduction condition—a lack of oxygen resulting in a smoky atmosphere that produces desirable glaze colorations. Unfortunately, the smoke which creates the desirable effects must pass out of the kiln into the atmosphere. Some cleaner fuels, like natural gas, LPG, and methane, can place carbon smoke into the kiln chamber with relatively little residue appearing out of the flue opening, but reduction can be introduced into the kiln at such a heavy saturation that a great deal of smoke will emerge from the flue opening. Pollution laws require that many industrial installations install auxiliary burners which will eliminate carbon or residue in the stack. It is interesting to note that some pottery kilns are specifically designed to include an auxiliary burner in the stack, but with the purpose of heating the stack in order to create a better draft through the kiln—the reverse purpose of an auxiliary burner to eliminate residue. The burner is turned on when the stack is cold, to start movement of heat through the kiln, and turned off after sufficient heat is moving up the chimney. At the latter stage, when the stack burner shuts off, smoke from the reduction firing passes out of the kiln. A stack burner like this could certainly be used for the dual purpose of inducing draft at the early stage of firing and burning off carbon before it escapes into the atmosphere during the later reduction stage.

One alternative to the auxiliary-burner system of eliminating excess carbon residue is to design a double-chamber kiln. In this kiln design, the primary heat source is in the high-temperature heat chamber, and this heat is then passed through a secondary chamber attached to the first, which is used to fire pottery at a lower temperature. The secondary chamber functions as an auxiliary-burner chamber, using heat that would otherwise be dispersed into the atmosphere. While reduction takes place in one chamber, the second chamber is relatively free of reduction by the time excess heat leaves its flue opening.

A very different approach to creating a reduction effect on pottery without the emission of smoke is that of inducting carbon dioxide into the heat chamber. Since CO_2, when vaporized, is relatively cold, the main problem is finding a means of introducing it into the kiln without substantially lowering the temperature inside. The chemical reaction which takes place when carbon dioxide is used in the kiln substantially simulates reduction changes on the surface of the glazes, and without the presence of smoke. But this approach is still in the experimental stage, with inconclusive results so far, and much more work must be done in this area to discover what the possibilities for success are.

Although not a secondary product of the fuel itself, salt vaporization out of the kiln flues is much more harmful as a pollutant than carbon because it is composed of sodium chloride and hydrochloric acid, which is highly damaging to the surrounding environment as well as to the kiln operator. Recently, experiments using substitute ingredients to create the same effect as salt vapor have been somewhat successful. The addition of sodium carbonate (soda ash) and sodium bicarbonate (baking soda) appear to provide similar results. (For more on this subject, read "Alternative to Salt Glazing" by Jeff Zamek in the June, 1973, issue of *Craft Horizons,* p. 38, and "An Alternative to Salt Glazing" by Richard Behrnes in the October, 1974, issue of *Ceramics Monthly,* p. 44.)

The thermal characteristics of ceramic-fiber materials will not be affected by carbon penetration into the walls or layering onto the surface. During low-temperature periods when carbon is building or during reduction at high temperatures, ceramic fibers remain inert and their insulating qualities do not change. When sufficiently high temperatures burn carbon away, ceramic fibers will appear white and clean as in their original state.

The heavier the fuel, the more residue results from combustion. Wood and coal, particularly soft coal, give off very heavy smoke. Sump oil (used crankcase oil) and No. 2 fuel oil also pollute heavily, while kerosene and diesel oil are relatively clean by comparison. Liquefied petroleum gas is heavier than air and will create thick carbonization during lower-temperature ranges of firing as compared to natural gas. Natural gas is known as one of the cleanest organic fuels available since it is mostly composed of methane, and methane gas is not only the cleanest of all organic fuels, but is virtually pollution free. The lightest of all organic fuels, it utilizes 98 percent of its substance in combustion. The composition of pure methane gas is:

Methane	89.61%
Nitrogen	9.61%
Carbon Dioxide	.23%
Oxygen	.55%

Its B.t.u. output per pound is 22,000 compared to 19,944 B.t.u. for propane and 19,680 B.t.u. for butane.

Clearly, methane gas has a very high heat content, one which would most certainly provide sufficient power to fire

a stoneware kiln to temperature. The utilization of the new materials discussed in this book and their characteristic of using heat in a more efficient manner than conventional insulating materials combined with a self-generating pollution free gas system would be the ultimate in self-sufficiency. Note that methane gas can be produced either from a small portable unit capable of providing fuel for a single pot cooker or from a large production unit which can furnish an entire plant for bottling storage tanks. Some researchers have estimated that the wastes from a family of five, if channeled into a 35-gallon airtight drum, would produce enough methane gas to furnish

10–1.

Methane Gas Production Flow Chart

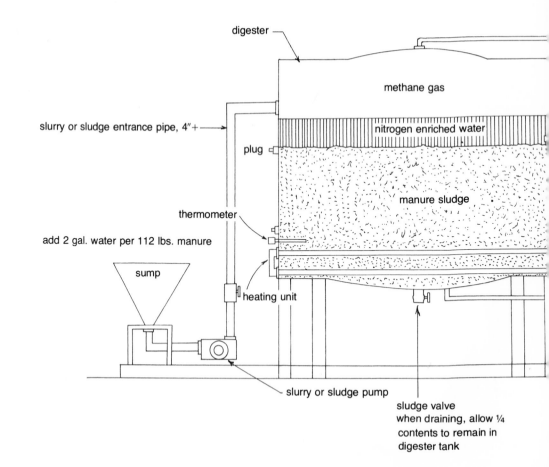

85,000 B.t.u. per day, and this would supply most of the basic energy needs for such a household.

The basic mechanism for producing methane is the "digester," and the basic organic development is called the "anaerobic process." The anaerobic process is the providing of a condition wherein bacteria can live in the absence of free oxygen. The digester is a container that will hold waste material and water combined into a sludge at a mean temperature range of 85 to 95°F. Although the sludge is normally thought to consist of manure and some type of vegetative matter, gas can also be produced by means of cactus juice or kelp from the sea. The flow chart for methane production (Fig. 10–1) gives information based on several reliable sources, not the least of which is L. John Fry, who drew on his personal experience developing and operating a complete methane plant in South Africa for six years.*

*His booklet, *Methane Digesters,* is available through The Mother Earth News, P.O. Box 70, Hendersonville, N.C., 28739, and additional information and diagrams can also be gotten by writing Harold Bate, Penny Rowden, Blackawton, Totnes, Devon, England. Mr. Bate became world-known when he developed an automobile that was fueled by methane gas made from chicken manure.

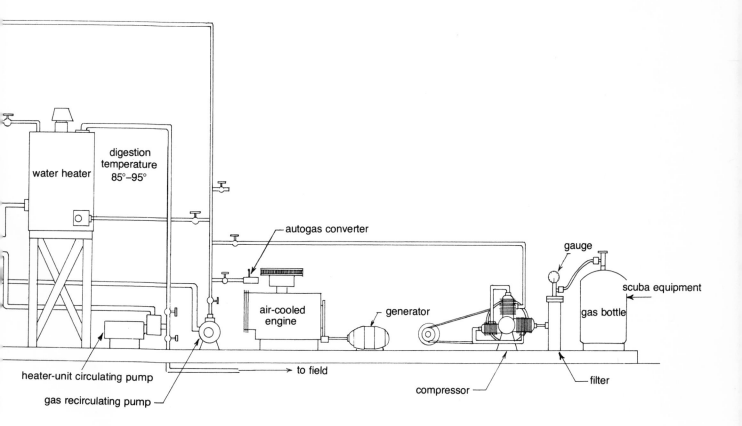

The production of Methane consists of two stages, which you can follow as you look at Figure 10-1:

1. Aerobic prefermentation. A compost pile of manure and vegetable material is made, the manure providing nitrogen and the vegetable waste providing carbon. The compost is wet with a hose and left exposed to air for approximately one week.

2. Anaerobic digestion. Compost is placed in the digester tank, and two gallons of water are added per hundred weight of compost. The temperature is maintained at 85 to 95°F. Methane production will begin in approximately one week. When gas production begins to drop (in approximately one week), the mixture must be replenished.

Union Carbide's solid waste disposal resource recovery system can develop four times the energy required to process the waste. Under the trademark of Purox System, this method utilizes pure oxygen to process solid waste material into a dry, clean-burning gas comparable to natural gas in its combustion characteristics. This gas, which may be used as a fuel gas, is virtually sulfur-free. One ton of solid waste material, when converted by this system, will provide seven million B.t.u.'s of fuel gas. It has a heat release per volume of combustion products of 95 B.t.u./SCF as compared to 89 for propane and 86 for methane.

Union Carbide's pilot plant was built in 1970 and processed five tons of solid waste a day. In early 1974, a larger PUROX System that processes 200 tons per day began operation in Charleston, West Virginia. Although the PUROX solid waste system is not yet practical for individuals, it is indicative of a reasonably new source of fuel that could become available in the foreseeable future.

Union Carbide has already established regional offices to handle interest in the PUROX System in and around densely populated municipalities where an abundance of solid waste is disposed of daily. (Fig. 10-2.)* Because of the availability of this waste in heavily populated areas, the demand for fuel gas is bound to grow.

*For additional information on Union Carbide's PUROX Systems, contact Solid Waste-Environmental Systems Department, Union Carbide Corporation, Linde Division, 270 Park Avenue, New York, N.Y. 10017.

It has become evident that extensive use, along with increased demand due to growing population, are depleting our natural resources at a frightening rate. It is also evident that alternatives are emerging and that some of these alternatives may prove markedly superior to the sources we have so long taken for granted and developed to such a high state of proficiency. The new materials described in this book are manufactured by a totally non-polluting energy: electrical energy. Energy for producing heat can be derived from hydraulic, wind, solar, atomic, or anaerobic power. Instead of being expendable, this energy can emanate from a constantly self-generating source. Conventional materials will become scarce as conventional energy sources become scarce; there simply isn't going to be enough firebrick in the years to come because conventional firebrick must be made by fossilized fuels. The fuels which are being used to fire the pottery are the same fuels that fired the bricks which make up the kiln.

Eventually the ceramic-fiber kiln will become the conventional kiln. Birds will construct their nests with ceramic-fibers, and rodents will insulate their burrows against the cold of winter with these materials (as one ceramic-fiber kiln owner in Woodstock, New York, has already seen them do).

Of all the self-generating sources of energy, solar energy is the most abundant. All other sources of fossilized fuels were originated from sunlight; without it, they would not have come into existence. Little research has been done on solar energy, yet some isolated experiments have successfully harnessed sunlight into concentrations of temperatures well over 8,000°F. This clearly indicates the possibilities of using sunlight as a direct source of energy for firing kilns. Ceramic-fiber materials are capable of containing 2,000 to 5,000°F. heat without difficulty. Surely, a means of using solar energy as the only source of heating power can be discovered.

10-2.

Inputs and Products of PUROX System*

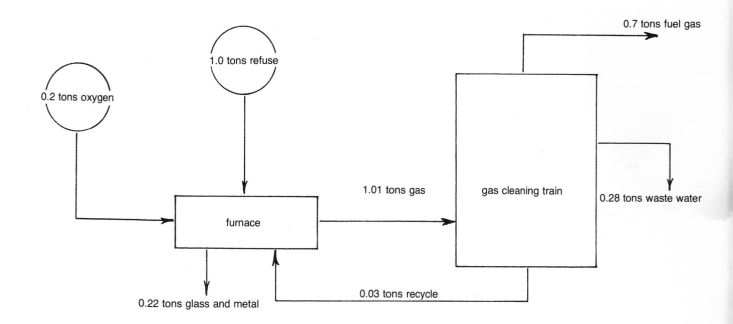

*Based on a drawing in Union Carbide's brochure F-3698.

Suppliers List

Ceramic-fiber Products
Babcock and Wilcox
Old Savannah Road
Augusta, Georgia 30903

Refractory Products Co.
500 W. Central Road
Mt. Prospect, Illinois 60056
(Ceramic-fiber blanket available in
small quantities)

Johns-Manville
22 East 40th Street
New York, New York 10016
District offices throughout the United States
and Canada

Union Carbide Corp.
P.O. Box 324
Tuxedo, New York 10987
District offices throughout the United States
and Canada

Carborundum Company
P.O. Box 339
Niagara Falls, New York 14302
District offices throughout the United States,
Canada, and the world

Thermo Engineering Co.
5105 Buffalo Avenue
P.O. Box 3935
Jacksonville, Florida 32206

Superamics
P.O. Box 8363
Madeira Beach, Florida 33738

Vari-Form-B and LDS Mixes—Boron Ceramic Fibers
Carborundum Company
P.O. 339
Niagara Falls, New York 14302
District offices throughout the United States,
Canada and the world

Magna 904
Magna Alloys and Research Pty. Lt.
Blackwall Point Road
Drummoyne, N.S.W. 2040
Australia

Colloidal-Silica Liquid
Nalco Chemical Co.
9165 So. Harbor Avenue
Chicago, Illinois 60617
(Request Nalcoag 1030)

Monsanto
800 No. Lindberg Boulevard
St. Louis, Missouri 63166
(Request Syton 200-IC)
District offices throughout the United States
and Canada

Monsanto Chemicals Ltd.
10–18 Victoria Street
London, SW1, England

Monsanto Australia Pty. Lt.
65 Bourke Road
Alexandria, N.S.W. 2015
Australia

DuPont
739 West Peachtree Street
Atlanta, Georgia, 30308
and
350 Fifth Avenue
New York, New York 10001
(Request Ludox colloidal silica)
District offices throughout the United States
and Canada

The Ransom and Randolph Co.
324 Chestnut Street
Toledo, Ohio 43691
(Request R & R NYACOL 1430 or 830)

Safety Solenoid Gas Cutoff Systems
General Controls ITT
801 Allen Avenue
Glendale, California 91201

Refractory Products
(Cast Refractories and Refractory and Insulating
Bricks and Related Products)

Babcock and Wilcox
Old Savannah Road
Augusta, Georgia 30903
District and international offices throughout
The United States, Canada and the world

A.P. Green Refractories Co.
Mexico, Missouri
District and international offices throughout
The United States, Canada, and the world

Denver Fire Clay Co.
3033 Blake Street
Denver, Colorado 80205

Mineral Wool Block
Babcock and Wilcox
Old Savannah Road
Augusta, Georgia 30903
District offices throughout the United States,
Canada, and the world

Mullite and Silican-Carbide Shelves and Posts
Norton Company
Refractories Division
Worchester, Massachusetts 01606

Carborundum Company
Refractories Division
P.O. Box 339
Niagara Falls, New York 14302
District offices throughout the United States,
Canada, and the world

Engineered Ceramics
Division of Sola Basic Industries
P.O. Box 1
Gilberts, Illinois 60136

Moldatherm:
Vacuum-Formed Kilns and
Furnaces
Lindberg
304 Hart Street
Watertown, Wisconsin 53094

Atmospheric Burners
Johnson Gas Appliance Co.
Cedar Rapids, Iowa 52405

Gas Appliance Co.
20909 Brant Avenue South
Long Beach, California 90810

Westwood Ceramic Supply Co.
14400 Lomitas Avenue
City of Industry
California 91744

Sodium Silicate
Fisher Scientific Co.
633 Greenwich Street
New York, New York 10014
District offices throughout the United States
and Canada

Nichrome Wire
Westwood Ceramic Supply Co.
14400 Lomitas Avenue
City of Industry
California 91744

Ceramic Suppliers
Arts and Crafts Colony
4132 No. Tamiami Trail
Sarasota, Florida 33580

Seeley's Ceramic Service
9 River Street
Oneonta, New York 13820

Helen Bennett Stoneware Potter
Box 8496
Orlando, Florida 32806

Western Ceramic Supply
1601 Howard Street
San Francisco, California 94103

W. E. Mushet Co.
725 Bryant
San Francisco, California 94107

Ceramics & Crafts Supply Co.
490 5th Street
San Francisco, California 94107

Leslie Ceramic Supply
1212 San Pablo
Berkeley, California 94706

Thorley Pottery Supply
1183 Industrial Avenue
South Gate, California 90280

Electro Refractories
18765 Fibreglass Road
Huntington Beach, California 92647

Pyro Engineering
200 South Palm
Alhambra, California 91801

American Art Clay Co.
Indianapolis, Indiana 46200

The Craftool Co.
1 Industrial Road
Wood-Ridge, New Jersey 07075

Kemper Mfg. Co.
P.O. Box 545
Chino, California 91710

Sculpture House
38 East 30th Street
New York, New York 10016

A. D. Alpine Inc.
353 Coral Circle
El Segundo, California 90245

Duncan Ceramic Supply
5649 East Shields
Fresno, California 93727

The Fenton Foundry Supply Co.
134 Gilbert Avenue
Dayton, Ohio 45403

George Fetzer Ceramic Supply Co.
1205 Seventeenth Avenue
Columbus, Ohio 43211

Standard Ceramic Supply Co.
P.O. Box 4435
Pittsburgh, Pennsylvania 15205

Rovin Ceramics Supplies
6912 Schaefer
Dearborn, Michigan 48216

Pyronics Inc.
17700 Miles Avenue
Cleveland, Ohio 44128

Robert Brent Co.
128 Mill Street
Healdsburg, California 95448

Newton Pottery Supply
96 Rumford Ave.
W. Newton, Massachusetts 02165

Rare Earth Mudworks
70 Merrimac Street
Amesbury, Massachusetts 01913

New England Ceramics & Kiln Supply
Shelter Rock Road
Danbury, Connecticut 06810

Hammill & Gillespie
Box 104
Livingston, New Jersey 07039

Ceramic Color & Chemical
Box 297
Brighton, Pennsylvania 15066

Stewart Clay Co.
133 Mulberry Street
New York, New York 10013

Minnesota Clay Co.
8001 Grand Avenue South
Bloomington, Minnesota 55420

Ceramic Data Book
Cahners Publishing Co.
5 South Wabash Avenue
Chicago, Illinois 60603

Index